MW00999886

As It Is Now Seen

Man: (Looks around at the laughing audience for support) Doesn't anybody *else* here want to know *when* this is going to happen?

Audience: Yes!

Ramtha: Master, time is an illusion. Do you understand that? *(Man nods.)* To predict an exact time frame is the greatest speculation there is, because many things must come together to bring about a specific change. So, to give you an exact hour cannot be done. But I can tell you precisely where the earth is *at this moment*—the state of your economy, the proximity of the growth of the sun spots, the intensity of carbon dioxide in your stratosphere, the warming of your planet, the eruption of volcanoes, and the pressure on the zippers.

The exact time cannot be determined. That is Nature's explosive moment.

***

ramtha intensive

change

the days to come

Sovereignty, Inc.
Eastsound, WA

RAMTHA INTENSIVE:
CHANGE, THE DAYS TO COME

Edited by Steven Lee Weinberg, Ph.D.,
Carol Wright and John Clancy

DISCLAIMER

ISBN 0932201-99-7
Library of Congress Catalog Card Number: 86-61219

FOR MORE INFORMATION:

For information about other books and audio and video cassettes presenting Ramtha's teachings, write to: Sovereignty, Inc., P.O. Box 926, Eastsound, WA 98245. 1-800-654-1407

For information about audiences with Ramtha, write to:
Ramtha Dialogues, P.O. Box 1210, Yelm, WA 98597. 206-458-5201

First Printing/September 1987

Book and Cover Design: Carol Wright

Sovereignty, Inc.

Box 926, Eastsound, WA 98245

Contents

RAMTHA INTENSIVE SERIES

Speaking through the body of JZ Knight, Ramtha has held more than 300 public audiences since 1978 in an effort to help awaken "gods asleep in the dream called mankind." Audiences presented prior to 1985 were called Dialogues because of their question-and-answer format. In early 1985, Ramtha began holding Intensives for the purpose of presenting more advanced teachings.

In 1986, Sovereignty published *RAMTHA*, the critically acclaimed bestseller which presents the cornerstones of Ramtha's teachings as well as the fascinating story of Ramtha's lifetime. Sovereignty's Ramtha Intensive Series extends and complements the material presented in *RAMTHA*. Each volume in the Series presents an edited transcript of a select Intensive, supplemented with related material drawn from Sovereignty's library of Ramtha's teachings. Although it is not necessary to read *RAMTHA* prior to reading the volumes in the Intensive Series, the reader is encouraged to do so for a fuller appreciation and understanding of the material presented in the Series.

An Introduction By JZ Knight

Before Ramtha begins Saturday morning's teaching, JZ Knight enters the hall, filled with an enthusiastic audience of over 800, who cheer and applaud her arrival. She climbs the speaker's platform and faces the audience.

JZ Knight: (Responding to the thunderous applause) Thank you! *(Looks over the packed ballroom in amazement)* Wow! Thank you.

I don't know how Ramtha does this! I'm coming out here to talk to you about fear, and I'm scared to death.

I'm coming out here to talk to you about fear, and I'm scared to death.

For those of you who don't know who I am, my name is JZ Knight, and I would like to welcome all of you to Denver. I am very happy that you arc here. I think this is the largest Intensive we've ever had.

We just came back from doing an Intensive in Tampa last weekend, and it was *wonderful*. The people who attended that Intensive were really a light to the whole hotel. The hotel people didn't want to see us go. I hope that this hotel will also be blessed because of your presence.

These next two days will be a very high-energy Intensive. Before I bring Ramtha in, I want to talk to you, as *myself,* about how this particular teaching affects me.

A lot of people don't know who I am or what I am. They just see a nice body and know that a magnificent entity comes through it and does wonderful things. And then there are a lot of people think who I'm a sacred cow, and *(audience laughs)*

I . . . I guess I should clarify that. They have a conception of me and my husband and my family. They think we go back home and live in ecstasy, and that we're excluded from all the things that everyone else is going through—all the runners and the dreams and emotions they embrace. I must tell you, that is not true. In our lives, we've been hard-pressed to understand a lot of things. The things that the Ram has been endeavoring to teach for the last eight years have also been manifesting in our lives. So we're also in a process of growing and evolving.

You know, you come and see the Ram, you walk out, you call him in the wind or listen to the tapes, and you get a lot of experiences. Well, contemplate his being there *all* the time. You're at the grocery store, and you're mad and impatient because you want to get through the line and hurry home to cook your pork chops, so you're judging a lot of people, and then, there *he* is.

I know a lot of you have gone through lots of things, and sometimes you feel like you're hanging on by the smallest thread, and that at any moment, you're going to fall. Well, we've been feeling like that for quite some time, not only with our growth process—and our hanging on to our limitations—but also with the process of bringing this teaching to everyone. So, on top of our own personal growth, we have the Ram, and we have these teachings, which are becoming international.

A lot of you are nervous, perhaps, because of what this Intensive is going to be about. We thought long and hard about a name for it, but the Ram said, "This is the name: 'Change: The Days to Come.'" How do you argue? How do you say, "It's not going to work, Ramtha"? So, the reason we have the title we do, is that this Intensive has to do explicitly with that title. But there's no itinerary here; that's up to Ramtha to manifest.

Our species has not always looked at the future with a delightful attitude.

You know, our species has not always looked at the future with a delightful attitude. We have usually looked at it as being very ominous and foreboding. So we thought carefully about this, because we did not want you to come to this Intensive because you're scared to death. That's why we said in the announcement, "Please, come here because you desire to *know*, not because you're scared and worried about what tomorrow is going to bring."

When I became aware of Ramtha, I didn't know who Nostradamus was. I didn't know about Edgar Cayce or Madame Blavatsky or a lot of other people who had prophesied the future. Because of my Christian upbringing, I knew about St. John the Divine and the Book of Revelation, and I grew up thinking that the world was going to come to an end. So, any time someone spoke about future events, it was something very frightful to me.

I grew up thinking that the world was going to come to an end.

As I began to evolve, I began to realize that we have been brought up with a basic understanding that toward the end of this century, it would be, you know, "Good-bye!" And so we were living in frustration, trying to justify why we're here and asking why should we go through all of this. I began to be aware of what the teachers were forecasting for this plane. It didn't look so good, and everyone seemed to be in alignment with that. I also began to realize that if you wanted to get someone's attention, all you had to do was tell them that the days to come are going to be horrible. That's why fear is the best seller in the tabloids; it's the bestseller in bookstores. So, we have been conditioned to be skeptical and uncertain about tomorrow rather than to embrace it.

Once Ramtha became a part of our lives, I began to understand something very crucial. He has always taught us that we're God, and that with our own knowingness, we have the capacity to change our future. We *can* change the next moment, simply by changing our attitudes. He really inspired my family by that truth, because we had been *living* like we were scared to death of tomorrow. He inspired us to live an attitude that would make tomorrow beautiful, joyful, and continuous in our lives.

Another important thing I began to realize is that you can't have knowingness if you are motivated by the attitude of fear. If people start talking about their knowingness of the days to

To truly have knowingness, you have to master fear, the emotion that has driven us all of our lives into living only for survival.

come, and the basis for their knowingness is fear, which *is* the common human attitude, their vision of the days to come will always be morbid, because it is coming from how they feel. To truly have knowingness, you have to master fear, the emotion that has driven us all of our lives into living only for survival, that has driven us into limitations.

As I began to understand that, I began to trust what Ramtha was saying. I realized that when I conquered fear completely, I would have a complete knowledge of what is to come for me and my family, because the knowledge wouldn't be coming from a state of fear but rather a state of love.

Now, I'm no longer afraid to die, because I now understand that when my life is finished here, when my dream here is complete, I go on and on, because I'm a forever being, like everyone else. When I mastered that understanding, I was not afraid to find out about tomorrow. My knowingness about the future came from a state of divine knowingness that was within me, from the god within me, that could come forward and be my light in my world.

What I realized and what I'm telling you, I didn't learn overnight. Ramtha has been in my life since 1977, teaching me very simple truths. And though they all manifested, it took a long time for Ramtha, being with me every day, to break through my barriers, because I clung and clung to my limited identity. But I have broken through many of them and I am coming to the other side.

These days that Ramtha speaks of are truly at hand for all of us. And it will take each of us, in an *individual understanding*, realizing this and mastering our fears and limitations so that we each become a light to the world. Now, being a light doesn't mean going out and preaching to everyone. It means being who you are, in complete ownership of yourself, and then living that truth from within outward. It is a becoming process. It's demonstrating that we have the power to *change*.

If we didn't have the ability to change, there would be no such thing as free will. But free will is the one law of God that is within us all. I'm telling you this because there are people here who are going to take the teachings from this Intensive, and they're not going to finish the end of the sentence which says, "You *can* change it." They're going to take the prophecies and go out and tell others, "Guess what! You've had it!" *Any* of it is changeable; that is the beauty of God within us. Whatever situation we've created, we can turn around.

They're not going to finish the end of the sentence which says, "You can change it."

I know this works, because I've been through a lot of change with Ramtha. I've received a lot of ridicule. A lot of antagonistic people have written to me, telling me they don't like what I do. They don't like what Ramtha teaches, so they take it out on me. That's all right now, but in the beginning it *wasn't* all right, because I was vulnerable to everyone's attitude. I had my insecurities, and I wanted so much to have *everybody* like me. You know what that attitude is like? You can have a thousand letters that say, "It was wonderful!" and then you get that *one* that says, "Buzz off!" If you're insecure, it only takes that one to bring you right down, and then you throw the baby out with the bathwater.

I had to learn what the truth and the light was for *me*. If I lived like everyone thought I should, I could never do what I'm doing, and I would be just as confused as I was before the Ram first came into my life. So I learned to change the desire to please all of you into my desire and knowingness to live my own light, to live my own truth, and to be sovereign with that. If I didn't do that, I would be a hypocrite to the truth that the Ram has been teaching, and a hypocrite to all of you. It has become my own personal vision and my own personal desire to wake up and come to the other side of this dream.

There are a lot of people at this particular time who are very critical of Ramtha and *this* Intensive. The criticism is not coming from the churches or from our government. It's not coming from my neighbors. It's coming from teachers in the metaphysical group. I'm talking to you about this because you're going to get a lot of runners about this; they'll all be waiting for us when we get home.

Ram has been criticized for holding this Intensive. But he is staunch, and he is sovereign. He does not deviate from the truth that we are God, that we create our own reality, and, as a result, we can *change* that reality. He doesn't placate us and say, "You're God, so you don't have to do anything." He doesn't tell us what we *want* to hear; he tells us what we *need* to hear. Because of that, he's sort of alone. But he is presenting the truth that we are all God, and that revelation is coming home to all of us. And he has never deviated from that simple, simple truth.

There were some people who were horrified that Ramtha would hold this Intensive on Change, because they could not be staunch enough to say what is, and then allow you to come into the realization of that. The Ram can because he loves you. I know, because he loves me, and I've seen that love with my family and with many other people. And his love isn't a conditional thing. He loves you regardless of whether you love him back. He has always been that way in my life. He's told me things I didn't want to hear, and I'd get mad and tell him, "Get out! There's the door!" (Well, he never uses the door.) Once, I didn't speak to him for six months because he had pushed a lot of buttons in me. But as much as I didn't like what he was saying, I knew it was the truth. And as much as I didn't want to *like* him, I respected and loved him enough to let him jolt me, to make me contemplate what I was doing and who I was. And eight years later, I'm beginning to see the fruits of that effort.

As much as I didn't like what he was saying, I knew it was the truth. And as much as I didn't want to like him, I respected and loved him enough to let him jolt me.

This Intensive and the ones coming up are working sequentially, and I want to explain to you why they're coming. This is the year of preparation. It is the year of knowingness and of decision, designed to take us from a helpless, futile, uncomfortable place, into having our own wisdom and our own knowingness so we will be able to have ownership of our future. It will give you the wisdom to cut through the fat, so to speak; to cut through all of the "but . . . but . . . but" and "I can't . . . can't . . . can't" and go right to the heart of the truth, and allow you to do with it whatever you want to do. And the end result? For those who have felt, contemplated and embraced it all, they will know that they are once again in control of their lives.

Now, the schedule for 1986 has been sort of a "Ramtha blitz." It takes a lot for us to go around the country doing these things, but it's worth it, because you need to know about the things that are coming. You need not be afraid of them, but you should know about them. Because from that knowledge, you can be in *full ownership* of the days to come, and you can take care of yourself and the god that is within you.

You may never see this sort of blitz again. I asked Ramtha, "How are you going to determine when your teaching is all finished here?" He said, "It will be finished when I come back to you, my brothers, and you know that we are equal in this understanding; when I don't have to say a word to you because you already know it; when you don't have the questions, the doubts, the judgments—all those tedious things that keep you here."

I asked Ramtha, "Are you just going to leave us then?" He said, "No," that he would see us through all of these things. That was comforting.

What the Ram does with all of us, including me and my family, he accomplishes through the love of God within us. He's doing this to bring us to the christ-consciousness. When that happens, what he came here to do will be finished.

What if all of you lit up? What if you all embraced your own christ?

Look at all of you in this room. What if all of you lit up? What if you all embraced your own christ? Can you imagine what would happen out there if all of you were masters in ownership and in control of your own destiny? if you had absolute love for the world and all people no matter whether they were from Russia or Libya? no matter whether it was your President or your neighbor? If you could love everyone unconditionally, it would *be* the "Second Coming of Christ"! It would *be* the new kingdom here on earth—because that consciousness would sustain it.

Ramtha didn't come here to raise an army. He didn't come here to get a bunch of people to follow him. He has never wanted that. If people start getting stars in their eyes, they just never come back. They don't *make* it back to these events because they didn't come here for what they *need* to know.

Ramtha is here, not among followers, but as one god to another god, bringing back and touching that truth within us that we've all squirmed in our seats about. We have copped out on our becoming. ''Well, I've been working on that little hang-up of mine for seven and one-half million years.'' The reason we don't want to work on our becoming is because we've found comfort zones.

Many of you hold on to fear because it's exciting.

Many of you hold on to fear because it's exciting. You want to hold on to it because it makes a good story. You want to hold on to it because it's your crutch. But as long as you lean on something that cloisters and limits you, you're never going to evolve into that magnificent entity that each of you are.

I honestly hope that all of you will take a look within yourselves to see why you came here. What *was* your motivation for coming here? Define it. Make a statement about it to yourself. You know, ''I came because I'm afraid,'' or ''I came because I don't know what's going to happen,'' or ''Somebody told me I should come here or else I'm going to die.'' Once you understand what you're wanting to hear here, you can look at it and own up to it. Whatever it is, *own* that motivation. Be true to yourself. Once you own that truth, then you're free of it; it becomes wisdom. Then, what the Ram will endeavor to teach you here, you'll be able to hear and own. You will have allowed yourself the opportunity to open up your *own* innate, wonderful knowingness—your *feeling*, your voice within—that will guide you through this life to the other side of the dream.

Ramtha isn't here to lay a ''heavy'' on you. He's here to tell you, as he always has in very simple, very explicit, very scientific terms, of a knowingness that allows you to reason things for yourself. He is going to tell you about the shadow *we* have cast before us, that *we* have created from our own attitudes. When you hear direful predictions, a lot of you will say, ''I was *afraid* these things were going to happen!'' But any time you react with fear, you add *to* what's going to happen rather than help change it and make it better.

Ramtha is going to tell us about the days that are coming. But you have to remember something grand. Inasmuch as we created the shadows that are now manifesting on our plane, we can also *change* them. And it only takes a *moment* to do that. When you've totally mastered fear, you can change your *whole* life.

Inasmuch as we created the shadows that are now manifesting on our plane, we can also change them.

Ramtha says it takes only one christ, one who has become the lord-god of his being, to be a light to the *whole* world. Now, when I was little, I thought about Jesus walking around "shining on." That was my reality, that was my truth. But I've realized that being a light is not that we have a spotlight that we shine out to everyone which says, "Look at me! I'm a christ!" It's not even *saying* that "I'm a christ." A christ is an individual who has mastered all of its limitations, has embraced the god within itself, and manifests God as god-man, the living christ. His *attitude* can lift the whole of the world, can lift all of social consciousness. His attitude allows us to see the truth of God in another living entity.

There is a tremendous amount of energy and love and understanding going out with this knowledge. Ramtha is not just putting knowledge in your head; he is touching "the christ within" with the simplicity of his truth, and the christ itself responds. It the christ within us that brings us to a state of knowingness. I know; I've embraced that concept; my family is embracing that concept. We're finding joy in our lives right where we are, regardless of the people who don't like me for what I do, or Ramtha for what he does. I've learned to love them and allow them, because loving and allowing are the greatest truths of all.

I wanted to share my understanding with all of you, and ask you to ask yourselves *why* you came, what was the motivating force or emotion behind your coming. Then take it and embrace it. If you do, everything that is going to be said in these two days will have a tremendous impact on you, and you will learn; you will learn how to know.

I appreciate your courage for coming here. And I appreciate and love all of you who have supported us and written to us. I haven't *really* thrown the baby out with the bathwater. I do appreciate your feelings, your support and truths, and the fact that you are with us in what we're doing.

I love all you guys. I desire for this Intensive to allow you to find a sense of freedom and light in your own life, and to know that you don't need *anyone* to tell you what to do—because you *already* know what to do.

Thank you again for coming. I'm going to take a little break and get Ramtha's "leased" body ready. I don't know when I'll see you again, but I hope I will be able to, sometime in the future.

You are loved, unbelievably, and that love is allowing you to be sovereign.

Just remember this: You are *loved*, unbelievably, and that love is allowing you to be sovereign.

And so, from my husband, myself, my family back home, and everyone at Ramtha Dialogues, may the god within you bless you and keep you forever. *(Blows a kiss)* So be it. *(Audience applauds, and JZ leaves the stage.)*

***

Saturday Morning Session May 16, 1986

Ramtha enters the hall wearing a simple white tunic that covers white pants. After climbing the stage, he studies the audience and then begins his address.

Ramtha: Indeed!

Audience: Indeed!

Ramtha: You, gathered in this august body, be that which is termed my beloved brothren. I, in this outrageous illusion, be that which is termed Ramtha the Enlightened One. I salute you. So be it!

Know you what ''indeed'' means?

Know you what ''indeed'' means? It is an ancient, wondrous word that holds *power*. It is the purity of a divine principle manifested into speech. It means ''in action,'' ''in movement,'' *indeed* ''in power.'' So, I greet you ''in power, in action''; indeed, in ancient love. And you respond ''indeed, indeed, indeed!'' It sounds wonderful, but it is far grander to *know* what that word means in your understanding. Now that you know, when you are a little short of help, you can ''indeed'' it into life!

(Picks up a glass of lemon water from a side table) Know you of that which is termed ''the bitter water''? It is a wondrous elixir. In its simplicity, it aligns the electrum of the body, and the body becomes greater aligned with the spirit. And so, for the moments that we spend together, you will be drinking a *lot* of bitter water. *(Toasts)* To Life!

Audience: To Life!

Life is the only reality, for it is the only thing that is constant and continual.

Ramtha: Life is the only reality, for it is the only thing that is constant and continual. Forevermore shall it be.

Now, know you that your face is only a mask? But through the god of your being, the light of your being that *holds* together the mass of your physical embodiment, all is known of one entity. The eyes, the nose, the lips, the hair—they are wondrous, but they are deceptive. The truth of an entity is that which *illuminates* him. Through that light, all is seen and known and understood.

Now, it is not important who *I* am. It is you learning of who *you* are that is important. It is not important what I look like or if I am a reality or not! What *is* important is bringing forth a grand understanding that allows you, through knowingness and courage, to perceive your own god. For that purpose, what will manifest this day and go with you when you leave this audience is a reflection of who you are. For that, be exceedingly pleased.

(Lifts his glass for a toast) To *you*, most *wondrous* entities, for your life will certainly change before this Intensive, as it is so termed, is finished. *(Drinks)* So be it.

Audience: So be it.

Ramtha: So you want "to know," eh? If there is anyone here who does *not* want to know, do leave this room this hour. *(Waits, but no one leaves)* Well, you're a hardy lot!

I listened to my beloved daughter in her desire to speak out "personal self." There is grand truth in what the entity says. But for you to know: What she has spoken is only truth when you *become* that principle within yourself.

Now, future: the *days to come*. There are a grand lot of you who have been ever so busy turning your heads backward and looking into some murky, smelly, remote past. You are searching for lives past, days past, correct? But where does that take you? What does that tell you of your *days to come*? Very little. Perhaps you are seeking validity to the notion that you lived once before to give you the assurance that you're going to live again. But looking to your past does not always do that. Because even though you greatly believe that you lived before, you are still perilously fearful that you might never do it again. You understand?

Though you search your past to find your identity, you shan't *ever* recognize it that way. Because all that you were before is only a small token of who you are *now*. And all the while you are looking backward, you are without a now; because as the now is happening, you are lost in the murkiness of yesterday, in an uncertain life, a life of groveling in the marketplace for survival—the thing that has *ravished* mankind for seven and one-half million years!

When you look to the past, how will you know the future when it becomes your now? How are you going to embrace that which is to come if your head is turned backward? You are never going to. You will only die in the pages of yesterday. You will die as an unremarkable entity, an unestablished entity, an insecure entity, only to seek another a life for another opportunity to evolve yourself and become grander and unique.

Know you the word "evolve"? *No one* evolves if they are backtracking. If you are looking to yesterday, you are not evolving; you are *stagnating*; you are only repeating a *very* sad story. Get it?

Audience: Yes.

Ramtha: To understand today is not to understand *yesterday*; it is to be aware of your feelings in *this* moment. And that awareness is unique within each of you, because that knowingness tells only *you* what is happening now with *you*.

All of you here, even those looking backward, create the horrors or the sublimity of tomorrow through your attitudes and thought processes in each moment of your now. So, if your now moment is engaged in contemplating a past life that was e'er so tragic, when you re-live it, you are re-creating that tragedy, *in emotion*, and that emotion will manifest to become your tomorrow. Do you understand? The past is *old news*. Life is *now*.

The past is old news. Life is now.

I desire for you to understand this at the beginning, for whatever you are embracing and however you are feeling in each moment affects the whole of the world. Whatever you think and embrace emotionally becomes the outward manifestation. Attitude creates the destiny of mankind. Your future is a result, in part, of the collective attitudes of all entities. And here, gods are caught up in the pettiness of limited attitudes, and those attitudes—*your* attitudes—have cast their shadows upon your plane, which is now in the slings and arrows of the beginning of its manifested plight.

Now, you *have* lived before. But however you lived, whether it was nobly or outrageously, does not matter. What *does* matter is who and what you are at *this* moment of your life. I am here to help you clear your senses so that you can take in *new* knowledge and a new understanding that will allow you to make decisions from *this* life and *this* wondrous moment *forward*. Get it?

Audience: Got it.

Ramtha: So be it!

Now, know you what Nature is? Hear you of the grand old gal termed "Mother Nature"? Nature is the wondrous continuum of birthing, called Forever. It is, unequivocally, the grandest reality of all realities, and it will, indeed, have a profound effect upon everyone gathered in this room; because without the platform of Nature upon which you live out your illusions, there *is* no future.

Without the platform of Nature upon which you live out your illusions, there is no future.

Many have spiritualized Nature into being; many have scientifically rationalized it into being. Well, they are both right. Nature is God, or Thought, realizing itself in *all* forms. Thought is the highest, because the basis of all life is Thought. Thought is God, the Is; it is the space that holds all of your solar systems in place.

What do you think space is? Nothing? But what do you think holds up your earth? Atlas? What holds up your sun? What allows the stars to be in profusion? What allows forever to be forever? It is space, called Is.

Now, I desire for you "to know"—not through speculation or some spiritual philosophy, but through a profound science of "isness." I desire for you to have something you can count on, and through which you can ascertain your destiny, easily.

How do you think your sun came into being? The big bang? Well, your scientists think so, because science cannot get beyond the infinity of that which is called the "Z particum." Hear you of the Z particum? *(Looks at the sea of puzzled faces)* Well, I have lost half of my audience!

The last letter in your hieroglyphics of common speech is Z, correct? *(Audience members nod in agreement.)* Now we are making progress! "Z particum" is a term used to describe the last known, highest revealed particle that was created at the moment of the big bang. Your scientists and your physicists do not know what lies *beyond* Z because they have limited themselves in common speech from A to Z! So, they cannot come up with anything thereafter. They are endeavoring to have knowingness, yet they are bogged down in their limited letters. But that which is termed the Z particum is the breaking of Light into a lower form.

The universe was not created from an explosion.

The universe, the sun, the earth—they were not created from an explosion. They were created from Space, the Knowingness, that which is termed Thought, the *forever* Is.

In the beginning, before there was a beginning, there was Thought. When Thought contemplated itself, it turned inward, and a realization occurred. That realization became Light. From Thought contemplating itself, Light was born. Light is the next principle of Thought.

This light *(pointing to the chandeliers)* is a very poor example of Light. This light is a *lower* electrum light. The greatest light is beyond your three-dimensional vision.

The Light created from Thought contemplating itself became Movement in your universe. That movement solidified itself at the moment of birth. At the moment of its birth, Light sparkled in Space, the backdrop of forever. It was Knowingness's first *adventure*, if you will. It is of that Light that all of the gods were born.

Know you that the continuum of Light is broken into light particums? For Light is the full manifestation of energy that is made up of the *vibrancy* of Thought.

So, from the *first* light was born the gods. And who were they? *You*—and all entities, seen and unseen, that have ever lived through the divineness of their souls. The gods are the greatest light of all. From *their* light the explosion of creativity occurred, because it is only from the dynamic force of you, the light particums, contemplating and creating like the Is once did, that a *lower* light form could be created. And in the lower light form, the Z particum is contained.

Creation began from the Z particum dividing into the X and Y particums to create *combustion*, gases, that which is called your suns. The suns gave birth to the planets by an explosion of *powerful* energy, which rotated around the sun in an explosive fission. As this energy rotated and moved into an orbit further away from the sun, it began to cool. As it rotated, and the more it cooled, the more hollow the planet became on the inside because the rotation and centrifugal force thrust everything that was in the core, the center, to the outermost perimeter. Only after it became hollow on the inside and cooled on the surface did the gods begin to make their homes here and to create, in the embryo state, *all* cellular mass. And *you* did it all.

Now, masters, this has been sort of a short re-cap of eternity, correct?

The "big bang" is called that only because your scientists don't know what happened *prior* to that. But the gods were first. From them, the creative element ensued, and it has been ongoing ever since.

The gods were first.
From them,
the creative element
ensued,
and it has been ongoing
ever since.

What did the gods create from? The Is, of course; Thought, of course. Thought is everlasting Life. Thought taken to its lowest form is called *gross matter*, which is made up of atoms. Each atom has a billion particums within it. Have I lost you? It's called *Infinite* Mind.

Once the Is contemplated itself, it went into itself, and life has been ever since. *And it always shall be*, forever and ever and ever.

Now, there is no such thing as the beginning of time. Only when man created and began to live by time did it become a reality. Time is one of the greatest illusions of all because it rules your lives, and yet it doesn't exist in the Is.

Now, let us talk about Nature. No man shall ever destroy Nature, suppress it or alter it. It is God, or Life, *evolving*. When Thought contemplated itself, evolution was born, knowledge was born. And that inevitable cycle will continue forever—in *spite* of the lot of you.

Mother Nature is evolving. It is Mother Nature who is birthing the planets. It is Nature who, through photosynthesis in your plant life, allows your dreams to manifest on this plane. Nature—the earth, the sun, the beauty of the enchantress moon, the forever stars, the wind upon the water, the seasons—*is* reality. Nature is the immutable law of God in its adventure into itself. It is not changeable by man. And if you attempt to war with it, it shall always be victorious over you, regardless of what you do.

Nature is the immutable law of God in its adventure into itself.

Now, your sun is important to you. It is the only one you're familiar with, correct? Well, you know your Way that runs with "milk"? There are billions of suns there. But your sun is all you need be concerned about, because it has *infinite* possibilities. And if it didn't come up tomorrow morning, wouldn't *you* be in a fine kettle of fish. Your sun is a young maiden that will never grow old because it is in a continuous life cycle that will go on, long after your memory has gone from this plane.

(Stopping to look at the flowers) Well, are these not jolly beautiful? They are indeed nature! And without the sun, these little lovelies couldn't perch themselves up here so arrogantly.

Now, the sun, in its core, is Thought reflecting into itself, which creates light; the light creates fission; and the fission creates the fire, the raw birthing energy. The great winds that prevail around the sun's grandiose light are called winds of the solar system. They are divine, and they carry light particums not only to your earth but to the farthest planet in your solar system.

The sun has a profound effect upon you and your earth. You are in a *tenuous balance* with its life, and yet few of you realize it. The light particums and the solar winds control your weather. If the sun is intact and in harmonious balance, your weather will always be in a harmonious balance.

The sun creates radiation that reflects off the face of the earth. Through the friction of particums in the stratum surrounding your earth, heat is created. That is why you are warm when you walk out into a sunny day. It isn't the *light* of the sun that warms you; it is the *friction* that warms you. Clouds are created in a *balance* from the solar winds and the friction of light particums hitting your earth. The clouds carry vapor from the oceans, cleanse it, and provide you with water.

Hear you of the term "sun spot"? Know you what it is? It is the explosion of Thought occurring. That is why it is so dark and seems to be almost an endless pit when viewed. From that spot, the eruptions of thought are coming into the fission of the X, Y, and Z particums.

In an eruption of "Thought becoming matter," the solar winds are at hurricane gusts. Every moment that eruption occurs and reaches *millions* of miles into the universe, you are seeing new energy exploding from Thought. You are seeing *creation*! The blackness, the hole, is "Thought realizing itself." It is so simple, yet everyone has looked for the complexity of why it does this. Well, it is simply your sun evolving to become more. Every moment it is spotting, it is becoming more and more.

Your sun is becoming spotted. It is fixing to have a bellyache. And these spots, these eruptions, are going to have a lot to do with you, who are of *tenuous* flesh and blood. Your weather conditions are already beginning to reflect the thought that is manifesting itself into a great spot upon your sun. Already your weather has become erratic and unpredictable. All you have to do is *look* and you will know that changes are coming in Nature. It is a *natural* cycle of evolution that is working *in harmony* with your earth plane.

All you have to do is look and you will know that changes are coming in Nature.

In the year that is coming, called in your counting Nineteen and Eighty-Seven, you are going to see a *huge* spot on your sun, with *huge* flares the likes of which your scientists have never seen before. This is a cycle in the life of the sun. With it comes drastic weather changes that will profoundly affect you who are *unprepared* for it.

Now, you must understand something about Nature and its cycles of change. Change is ev-o-lu-tion, the continuous *ripening* of Life, the expansion of Life *every moment* it is expressed. And in each new moment of its expansion, Life will be grander and grander and grander. Change is to move *forward* into today and that which is called tomorrow. It is purposeful. It is continual. It is the premise of demonstrated forever. And it will go on and on and on and on, for it is God in its immutable law called Nature.

Now, the sun isn't spotting because it's ticked off at you. It is not angry, mad, or upset with you. It is not looking at you and snickering, ''Watch this!'' Your sun is simply in its *natural* cycle of expansion. It is *evolving*; and, as a result, your earth plane is going to react to that evolutionary process.

Every time your sun has been disrupted by its eruptions with their solar winds, you have experienced a drought in your history. Correct? Well, what is coming upon your plane is a drought. We are talking about *thirsty soil*, soil lacking the nourishment that allows wheat to expand from a seed to the full birthing of its beautiful, golden stalks.

What is coming upon your plane is a drought. We are talking about thirsty soil!

Your country has been a savior in feeding many people in this world, correct? So profoundly abundant has it been, that many farmers have left the land. Well, always before the sun becomes spotted, you are in the greatest balance of all. That is why in certain areas of your earth, crops are more abundant than they've ever been. It is Nature's way of providing you with excess to see you through times that are about to become lean. Get it?

Audience: Yes.

Ramtha: Now, listen to this: Know you when you are hungry before dinner, and it has always been so *convenient* to drive and pick up foodstuffs? (I've never seen anything like it! We always had to halt for days just to prepare a decent luncheon!) You never really think about where your food comes from because you can always run hurry-scurry to the market

You are oblivious to what's going on under your feet, in your heavens, in your soil.

and *squeeze* that bread! Fresh! Fresh! Fresh! So, you don't think about Nature. You don't realize and appreciate this grand, fundamental reality. You are too caught up the convenience you have created, and you have become soft in your buttocks and bellies. You have become lazy entities who are going to be *unprepared*. You have wrapped yourselves up in your own illusions, your own problems, and you concern yourselves with *petty* things. Petty! You are oblivious to what's going on under your feet, in your heavens, in your soil. You are limited people because your vision has become very constricted.

In the latter part of 1987, you are going to be besieged upon the land because there will be no water, and your ''bread basket'' is going to become depleted. Your abundance will go very rapidly because you are feeding everyone else in the world. Understand?

Nature, the evolutionary processes, is in harmony with *everything*—except you who are terrified because you cannot *imagine* living off the land, because you have become so used to going to your super-super-super-supermarkets and picking something up.

(Sips a glass of water and holds it up) Better drink it! *(Toasts)* To everlasting water!

Audience: To everlasting water!

Ramtha: Masters, so that you know what I have told you is a truth, get out of your petty little boxes and go do research at your libraries. Talk with your scientists. Ask them, ''When was the last cycle of droughts caused by the sun?'' Do it! Then you will understand that this knowingness has now reached many of your people, who are also endeavoring to communicate this truth to you.

Now, understand this: The time of the drought *can* change. It can be at a later time. But it *is* coming; it is already effective. This is not something to be angry about. It is simply Nature evolving. But perhaps, masters, you should look at your cupboards and assess how in harmony with Nature you are. If you are in harmony with it, you understand its cycles, embrace it, and you are prepared. If you are not in harmony with Nature, you will scuttle about wondering why God has brought this plague on you (which is your natural reaction: to blame everyone else except yourself). Well, you can squiggle and cry all you want to, but it will do no good.

So, what are you going to do about the drought? Whatever you do *now* is what you are doing about the drought.

This drought is one thing that is coming in the days to come, but it is only a *small* thing that is coming. We have not yet talked about what *you* have created and its effect on your days to come. We are talking first of Nature, because without Nature you will *have* no days to come! Understand?

Without Nature, you will have no days to come!

Audience: Yes.

Ramtha: Now, you have been looking for ''divine'' inspiration. You have been running to teachers, burning incense, chanting, consulting ''multudious'' guides, trying to decipher your dreams and visions, reading the leaves in teacups. You've been asking those who have set themselves up as ''knowing entities'' all about those small things, like: ''What of my relationship?'' ''What of my career?'' ''Can you change so-and-so's mind about about me?'' And they're glad to give you answers; all you have to do is ask them. And if you ask ten thousand people, you will have ten thousand *different* answers!

You have been looking for *the* Truth. You have been looking at headlines that say, ''Psychic at Large: The Truth.'' Bah humbug! The truth *is*, you're looking in the wrong place! Because where are your teachers and your guides going to be, entities, when you're hungry? Hmm? They may give you food for *thought*, but that really isn't going to cut it when the drought comes. *(Audience laughs.)* Well, it is a truth! *(Picks up his glass and toasts)* For you to know.

Now, one of the grandest teachers of all is the ant—you know, those pesty little creatures that are intent upon snatching away the deli from your picnic or the crumbs you carelessly left in your kitchen. In my days, I watched ants with great love and respect, and I saw such a grand *intelligence* from such a minute, determined entity. If they were people, they would have all become God and ascended long ago, because *they* don't have any hang-ups!

Now, we are talking of teachers in Nature; we are talking about the *real* thing. These entities are delighted when the first roast of a spring sun begins to thaw and melt the winter snow. They become very busy excavating themselves right out of their hovels to bask in the wonderful warmth, in the rejuvenation of another spring to be lived. Straightaway, these wondrous creatures begin cleaning up their house. They clean out their closets, so to speak, and then they begin their collection of foodstuffs for the next year. And they work *in harmony*, harmonious existence.

Masters, if you take a town and an antbed, and you put them side by side, *which* do you think would work together most harmoniously? I assure you, the ants would. In the town, there would be cursing and yelling and fistfights breaking out, because you have proven through your times that you can't work together. That is all right; you'll have your chance to change this.

You have proven through your times that you can't work together. That is all right; you'll have your chance to change this.

The ants labor and play and are joyful. They store food all spring, summer and fall, for they certainly know that the great white silence will return to the land. They prepare for it. They do not *do* it out of fear, but out of a *natural* desire to survive. They do not *hate* the winter; they *understand* the winter, and they know how long it will last. They take care of themselves and they prepare. When spring comes again, they will have survived it all—and they *know* that spring *always* follows winter. In their knowingness, the ants are fully aware of the sun and the earth and their evolutionary processes. They are great teachers for you. Yet how can you ever bring yourself down to an ant's level when you are endeavoring *so* arduously to become *so* exalted!

Now, for the lot of you, I will send you some runners, and the runners will be ants. And if you spray the little devils into oblivion, you will have just slaughtered your great teachers!

I am sending these runners to you. And you will find them

in the most *unexpected* places. I desire for you, my brothers, to watch them and follow them. I know you are larger than they are, but they are swifter and more clever and more determined than most of you. Perhaps, in watching them and in understanding this with great humility, you will gain the virtue of *their* noble attitudes.

I desire for you to watch what they're doing. If you say, "Oh, I won't do that!" I'll send them to you *one thousand-fold*. So, you won't be able to help but watch. I do this because I love you.

Observe them. They *are* divine. And they'll know you're watching. They will go about doing what they always do, but with an audience. Let them teach you something, emotionally, about being prepared. When you live liken unto the ant, you are living in harmony with God and the enigma called Life. So be it.

Audience: So be it.

Ramtha: How much food do you have in your pantries? How long will it last? Two days? Three weeks? If you do not have enough provisions for *two years*, you are going to run perilously short. The sun spots, for the most part, cause droughts which have consistently lasted for at least two years in counting. It is through this process that the earth rejuvenates itself. To prepare yourselves in this way is not adding to fear in social consciousness. The ant does not *add* to fear. It adds to the harmony of Nature because it *is* in harmony; it is in alignment with what it *knows* to be a truth.

If you do not have enough provisions for two years, you are going to run perilously short.

Surviving is not difficult. It is a *sublime* thing that need *not* be a hardship. When you are in flow with Nature, you never have to *struggle* to survive because you are just "in the flow." If you are scrambling to find shelter and something to eat, you are at a place of *base* survival. You are working *against* the flow because you have not been in harmony with the truth, the movement, the cycle of Nature.

Is this a fearsome truth? Is it "doom and gloom"? How could *Nature* be doom and gloom? How could it be anything but admirably *beautiful*? It has always been so. But if you fight it, if you are against it, you will not win, because Nature is *forever*; it *knows* it is forever, while you are still tenuous.

To prepare is not a foolish thing, it is a *wise* thing to do. You who have grown lazy in your minds and in your backs, who have walked away from the country and your small pieces of land to embrace your cities (because that is the consciousness that you *want* to be in), you are going to be in great, *great* peril.

If an entity has even a small piece of land, he can grow his staff of life and he can nurture and preserve that which he grows. That will carry him through even the most arduous of circumstances. Then he is free! But *you* are not free. When your drought comes and the baker doesn't bake the bread because the wheat isn't there, because the wheat didn't grow, because the rains weren't there, how are you going to have bread? Do you even know how to bake it? Do you know how to grow it and to glean the wheat from the chaff? You *don't* know, because you've never *had* to know. You are no longer in love with the land, only with *convenience*, which says a lot about what you think about time.

Know you who inherits the kingdom of heaven? Know you, masters, who inherits the state of mind termed "Superconsciousness"? It is *not* the intellectual! It is not those who worship complexities! It is the *meek*, those who are *humble* within their beings, who are close to the earth and work harmoniously with it, who are in *alignment* with it. They are the meek. They are the ones who know. They are the ones who put up provisions because they *love* what they are. It's as simple as that. *(Looks over silent audience)* And they do not *play* with the illusion called death.

You are going to have the chance to choose.

There are many of you in this audience who are desiring enlightenment. Yet you are vacillating between that desire and your fantasies of death and dying and suicide. You are going to have the chance to choose. You are going to find that those visions and fantasies will flee from your being, because there will be a nature within you that will connect with you; it is called the desire for *survival*.

The meek are *always* prepared, not because they are anticipating a great calamity, but because they love themselves and others enough to always be sovereign and never at the mercy of *anyone* else.

You are not free people! You think you are, but that is your illusion in your little boxes.

You are not free people! You *think* you are, but that is your illusion in your little boxes. You know your box? Tidy, clean, immaculate, scrubbed, no odors.

How free *are* you? If it ever happened in your cities that there was no food in their markets (and it is going to), who are you at the mercy of? If you have not grown and secured your own food, what sort of freedom do you have? Who is going to give you a handout? Are you understanding what I am saying? *(Audience nods.)*

Nature is a wild, *free*, ever-moving entity-thing-self. On this plane, only Nature exhibits *complete* freedom. You exhibit complete *enslavement* because you depend upon things *outside* of you.

Why has it been said that the meek shall inherit the earth? What about all of *you* wonderful entities?—you who are so grand, who know *so* much, who can quote anything and everything. Why doesn't the meek include you? Because they are in harmony. And they don't profess anything other than "It is God and Life." They don't argue against you; they just *allow* you, for they understand that you have your own truth. They are simple in soul, humble in spirit. They are without complexities. They are without "intelligent conversation." They are close to the simplicity of the line, which is *Omnipresent Mind*. They are the achievers. They are the salt of the earth. *They* are going into Superconsciousness because *they* are preparing for it.

You can take this knowingness and reconcile it any way you want to. You can make all the excuses you want, from now . . . until 1987. You can find all the reasons why this *shouldn't* be a truth. That is all right. Those who know it, *know*; they feel it! They are watching the weather. They are *feeling* Nature. They are walking out into the wind. They are looking into the heavens *beyond* beyond. They are watching the burst of the beautiful morning. They *know* it. No one *told* them; they just knew. *It is their god speaking within them.* They are in harmony with their knowingness, and, because of that, it is they who will see Superconsciousness. That is simply how it is.

Now, your cities. They are seductresses. They are desirous of everyone to be there, yet love none who are. What would you reason about your cities in the days to come? Contemplate this with common, simple reasoning. Why are they not advantageous places to be in the days to come? Reason it! *No fields.* All turnpikes. There are hovels on top of one another, and the only thing that grows there are baskets of flowers.

Where does their food come from? Where does their water come from? *Where*? Reason this out; then you will understand why the city is not an advantageous place to be a part of. And the cities are going to be the first to spew forth diseases and the plagues. This is not ominous. It is simple knowingness and simple reasoning.

The days to come are loaded with many surprises. But they are surprises only for the *un*knowing, the *un*prepared, the ones who do not want to listen because it is too big of a deal to do anything about it.

So, where do you get two years worth of foodstuffs? Well, you have bountiful markets, don't you? Be bountiful in your acquisition from them. You have wonderful ways to preserve things. Go and secure however much you want. You will know when it is enough. Put it away in a clean, *clean* place.

If you are living in the city, you are in for big trouble.

What of your water? If you are living in the city, you are in for *big* trouble. If you are living on the simple earth, drill a well, find your water, and *have it there*. In my times, women would go to the river or to the well with their grand urns. It seems like a primeval way to do things, correct? But our women had broad shoulders, strong legs, firm hips, and the lot of them were *very* healthy. Make your wells so that water is accessible to you. Understand?

Audience: Yes.

Ramtha: Now, know you what electrum is? It light that has

been lowered into an electrical field of negative/positive energy. That is what creates the electricity that you plug into. Know you what it is to "plug in"? How many moments only this morning did you plug in? Hmm? Well, if your electricity wasn't there, I dare say you wouldn't have any curls on top of your head. And many of you would not have clean teeth, because if you couldn't plug in, it just wouldn't happen. Well, look at that. Reason that for a moment.

Electrum is a wild force that is *everywhere*. A brilliant, *simple* entity with vision and foresight discovered the way to harness it. Unfortunately, you have given up your sovereignty because you have become dependent upon it for your survival and enjoyment. Well, in Nature, electrum is a prevalent energy. There will come a day, very shortly in your time, when all you will need is a lightning rod to harness the magnetic energy of your northern and southern regions. You won't need to "plug in" at all. You will have something available to you that will allow you to be even more sovereign. The meek will be the first to know about this because they are *simple* enough to *reason* it.

Learn to be sovereign. Learn to be prepared. Find a place where you feel one with life and go forward. If you don't want to do that because it's too much of a problem, so be it; you're still loved. But now you know.

Learn to be sovereign. Learn to be prepared. Find a place where you feel one with life and go forward.

Now, the earth. What effect do the sun spots have on the earth? Obviously, if weather is affected, so are land masses. So, the earth is *also* changing.

For a long time in your counting, you have been expecting that "the great earthquake" would be coming. Correct? *Who* said so? Did *you* know that, or did somebody tell you that it was so, or did you read it in some great book?

What does the "great earthquake" mean? Does that mean one liken unto the quake that "did in" Atlantis? I have news for you. Atlantis was *not* done in by the *earth*; it was done in by the people who inhabited it. Because of their arrogance and stupidity, they caused a great valley filled up with water to create what is now a great ocean.

You know about many things, but you are ignorant about that which supports your evolution.

The earth has *always* been evolving, from the moment it was birthed into the cradle orbit of the sun until it reached this delicate orbit where, through photosynthesis, you could have green, you could have oxygen, you could have all of the elements for life. Your earth is a grand place to be, but what is your knowingness of it? What is your *knowingness* of Nature? You know about many things, but you are ignorant about life, that which supports *your* evolution. Well, you need to know the changes that are, at this moment, on the threshold. You need to know the dynamics of an evolving earth, because they are most definitely going to affect your future. You must understand that your earth is *moving*, it is *changing*, it is *evolving* and becoming grander. There is no thing in life that does *not* evolve.

Now, your earth has "zippers." I use the term "zippers" because I once saw a man who, instead of dropping his loin cloth, simply at his sweetest convenience pulled the little thing and it went zipping right down; thus he was able to relieve himself without undressing. A *wondrous* invention. It allows you to get into your pants, and then you just zip it up to fit! (Sometimes it doesn't fit, but you squeeze it in anyway!) *(Audience laughs uproariously.)* So I have taken the word "zipper" and I use it to describe what you call "fault lines," an ominous term which, when spoken, creates fear and uncertainty amongst many of you.

There are zippers all over your earth. Your earth is laced with them to allow the earth's crust to move, to allow the planet to expand. The zippers are the earth's "breathing points," and they will always run along those earth planes or continental lines that are most involved in movement.

Know you that your continent is moving? It is. Know you that all the shelves and plates of your earth's crust are moving? They are all in motion, even this moment that I am speaking to you. You should understand this, because in the days to come you're going to reflect on what you've learned here—because you're going to experience it! The earth is getting ready for a change, a new appearance, a new look, its *ex-*

panded self.

Your earth has been evolving and it will do so forever. Why do you think your continents have moved like they have? And where have those continents of ancient times gone? They are under the ocean. But life has come forth from the center of your oceans. In the center of your Pacific Ocean, your Atlantic Ocean, your Northern and Southern seas, there are great cracks in your earth. From those cracks, lava is continuously coming up. Know you what lava is? It is *future ground*. The lava is being created, and it is expanding your earth every moment. The earth is recycling itself through what your scientists call "plate tectonics." The plates are being formed in your ocean floor and they are moving according to the polar pull, the magnetic fields. At the present moment, the plates that have been created at the bottom of your seas are now moving toward your coastline, which is putting pressure on the zipper. As a result, the land masses of what is called your Pacific Coast are now in a movement thrusting northward.

Now, your ominous prophecies of "the great earthquake" have loomed over the earth, and many have been afraid that California would fall into the sea. But the ocean floor is moving *toward* California. So, what would it fall into? Where would it *go*? Arizona?

Know you that which is called Mexico? Its land mass, as well as that of California, is on a northern trek; they are moving *north*. They are not going to break up and fall into the ocean. Certainly, the waves from the zipper's movement are going to do away with many wonderful homes that were built so close to the sea for that wonderful view. (They are going to get a *grand* view!)

The earth, in harmony with the sun, is going through its evolutionary processes.

The earth, in harmony with the sun, is going through its evolutionary processes. It is creating *new* earth, which is in harmony with the New Earth of Superconsciousness and a new mind, a new understanding. Everything is working in balance. The continental shelf is now *pressing* against your shores. New lands will surface in your oceans; the birthing of them will be most prevalent. Your quakes *will* continue, and your mountains will continue to blow their heads off.

Now, what are volcanic mountains for? What is the purposefully designed greatness of them? Are they just an enigma of Nature? No. They are "steam valves." They vent the steam and the pressure that build up in the crust of your earth. When the pressure needs to be let off, they blow their tops, and everybody thinks that an ominous, dreadful thing has occurred. But don't you know what the matter is that the steam spews into your stratum? It is the earth's fertilizer, and wherever it falls upon your land, grand things will come up from it. That is what creates new earth on the outermost surface of your planet.

Earthquake activity will continue, and there *will* come a great quake. But it isn't *The* Quake. There is never The Quake, as it were; there is only evolution. The pressure is building up, and movement is occurring. The earth masses are moving along your zippers, or fault lines. You'll soon find out for yourselves where they are moving to.

This expansion is called plate tectonics. It is the new earth coming forward. It is the earth rejuvenating herself. Accept it.

Now, there are many entities who have sought to be close to the sea for its invigorating nature, its forever mobile essence, its healing spirit. Though it has, indeed, been a grand place to be, it will be no longer, because the earth is moving. So if your hovel is on the beach, know that it's going to be washed away. If you are wondering why this will happen, it isn't because God doesn't love you; it always has and always will. You created it by not reasoning with the flow of Nature and being in harmony with it.

In the days to come, seek dry ground, higher ground, away from the oceans.

In the days to come, one should leave the beaches and seek higher ground. If you have perched yourself in a hovel that is sitting on a zipper, you would be well-advised to pack your belongings and go somewhere else. You may find many reasons why you shouldn't do this. "Look how much I paid for that place! And it's got such a grand view! I love it here!" If that is your priority, then stay. But you won't love the view that is coming nearly as much as you love the present one. Do whatever feels right, but know that your earth *is* moving.

In the days to come, seek dry ground, higher ground, away from the oceans. Allow Nature to move. Allow her to create. Be *one* with it. Do you hear me? Is that a dreadful thing to hear? Understand and embrace this knowingness, this wisdom. Then you are in the flow of life. So be it. *(Raises his glass and toasts)* To Life!

Allow Nature to move. Allow her to create. Be one with it.

Audience: To Life!

Ramtha: Forever and ever.

Audience: Forever and ever.

Ramtha: Now, I desire for you to experience the trembling of the earth. So be it. *(Audience laughs nervously, and Ramtha joins them.)* Gotcha! I know what you're thinking. "But, master, if you love me, you shan't *ever* want me to experience that. I *know* what it is like for the earth to tremble." Not *now* you don't! So I desire for you to feel what you have always taken for granted, that was always there, that was a "no thing" to you, just so much crushed up rock. I want you to *feel* your earth's life for a moment. I want you to see the *power* of Nature for a moment. I want you to feel what it feels like to be *awakened* into stark reality. And when it is over, you'll want to fling yourselves upon the earth and give it grand kisses.

When the earth shakes, will you worry about your hairstyle or whether you brushed your teeth? How about your relationships? How about Saturday night?

A moving earth allows you to put everything into perspective, eh? And for those who are evolving and becoming God —finding that unequivocal majesty within themselves—this will be a wondrous experience and a grand teaching to clearly bring that realization home to you. Because at that moment, nothing else will matter except what you are experiencing. Then you will realize how *tenuous* you are and what is *really* important. Get it?

Audience: Got it.

Ramtha: So be it! You're going to have exciting days!

Your earth is God. It is *love*. It is *alive*. It is moving, it is volatile. The earth, plate tectonics, volcanoes, tremors, tidal waves—they are God expanding, moving, becoming *more* of itself, the reflector called Life.

Now, the Eastern seaboard. Are you aware of where that is? Entities there have thought for the longest time that they were living in "the" place. They thought that only California was going to go under, while their sublime consciousness would prevail. Well, wake up!

Your Eastern seaboard is *man's* contribution to the events that are coming to pass, for it is the industrial side of your continent. There, your air has become treacherous and poisonous. You are killing your forests, your fishes, and your foodstuffs. You are killing the earth. Nature, which is continually evolving to right itself and make itself anew, is experiencing a great and deep sore on your Eastern seaboard. It is *suffering*, greatly. In the days that will come, you will find your earth moving on your Eastern seaboard, even in your Midwest. You will see storms that will unleash a violence that you have never seen before. They will come from a place called the Dead Horse Drones in your Atlantic Ocean. The storms are called hurricanes. Know you what they are? They are coming in *profound* fury, because that is the only way that Nature, in its endeavor to heal its wounds, can clean the air and wash away the debris. And those storms are going to become more unpredictable.

Grand industrial plants are going to fall under the violence of Nature, for their drains are poisoning the water and polluting the great seas; and that which is in a delicate balance, which is lovely and beautiful, is becoming no more—because of *convenience*.

In the days to come, Nature will heal its wounds so that it can go on. It will get rid of that which is hurting it. Nature heals and moves forward.

Those are the things that are coming to your east and your west. In the days to come, Nature will heal its wounds so that it can go on. It will get rid of that which is hurting it. Nature heals and moves forward. These things are happening not because Nature doesn't love you. They are happening because Nature is a forever, immutable law, and it must take care of itself. Understand?

The people of my own land [India/Nepal], they will begin to endure the earth's trembling. That which is called the "high peaks of God" will get even higher. Cathay [China] and the Land of the Rising Sun will experience *great* movement in the earth from the shifting of the earth plates. Once dormant volcanoes will become alive and well. It is Nature "becoming." Man must know and understand that.

Hear you of the prediction of a nuclear holocaust? Know you what that is? The unleashed fission of energy; and once it's out there, you can't get rid of the radiation. Hear you the term "nuclear winter"? It is when the stratum becomes choked with dust and debris and radioactive fallout, and the sun can no longer find itself onto this plane. If that were to occur, you would certainly have another ice age. But man shall never destroy this plane. There shall never be a nuclear war. It is not going to happen—regardless of the prophets and their desire to bring forth another war. These prophets want to be right, at the expense of the whole of the world and all of Nature. They want to see it happen so they can say that their truth came to pass. Well, they are going to be brought down.

These things that I have spoken of are not signs of the ending of life; they represent the *continuum* of life. They are Nature, Life, God, being revealed. It is "the time of the meek." It is humanity awakening.

These things are not signs of the ending of life; they represent the continuum of life.

There shan't be a nuclear winter. And the earth is not going to split apart. Nor will it turn upside down on its axis. Why would it do that? Your magnetic poles *do* change; their electrical energy switches from negative to positive. But the earth does not have to flip over to do it! It simply does it. It is Life; and through that enigma, called power and energy, it rejuvenates itself.

If you are still certain that you are going to have a nuclear war, think on. If you are certain you are going to have an ice age because you hate to take back your words, freeze in it! If you wish to believe that the earth is going to flip over on its axis because someone said that Mercury was in retrograde, go for it! But these things are never going to happen, and that's wonderful!

Nothing shall ever destroy this planet. Ever! So be it. *(Toasts)* To Mother Nature.

Audience: To Mother Nature.

Ramtha: I am giving you an educational process of common reasoning that allows you, if you *want* it to, to learn how to have common sense, which *is* simplicity. To learn and embrace the physics of defined Nature is a grand and enlightened thing to do. To understand your plane is utterly important in the process of becoming God, because you do not become *without* this plane. You cannot learn these things through chants; they are a no thing. Rituals are a no thing. Your guides and teachers are a no thing because they are *not* going to walk in your shoes. Enlightenment is *knowledge*. It means "to be in knowledge of." To be God is not to be a cloistered, blind, superficial, spiritualistic, dogmatic entity! That is to die! To become enlightened is to embrace *knowledge*, to wake up to a grander understanding that encompasses all life. To become enlightened doesn't mean that you plug in and light up! It means that you *know*. With knowingness, you have absolute freedom and you can make any move.

To understand your plane is utterly important in the process of becoming God, because you do not become without this plane.

This that I teach you about Nature is vitally important, because many things are happening in Nature that need to be embraced and understood. With this knowledge and your *compassion* for life, nature and the elements, you are going to flow into a state of being that you have not yet the mind to imagine, the vision to see, or the feelings to embrace.

In these days to come, in this change, the earth is vitally important if you are going to see any days at all. How Nature is with you and how you are with it is going to determine whether your illusions, your nightmares, and your fantasies are important or not—*and* whether they're going to manifest.

Do you *know*, masters, that you are doing away with oxygen in your stratum? And, since you're breathing animals, what are you going to breathe? Do you know that you are poisoning your environment? *(Audience members nod.)* You *do* know that. Then *why* are you plugging into electricity that

If you know these things, why haven't you changed them?

is being supported by a *primeval* energy source that is now threatening Europa and parts of the Ukraine? [referring to the aftermath of the Chernobyl accident] If you *know* these things, *why haven't you changed them*?

When one becomes truly "in knowledge of," he is spurred from a noble adventure within him to *change*. You cannot say you *know* these things without changing them. Understand?

Audience: Yes.

Ramtha: Masters, it is *you* who have created the things that are destroying your very existence here. Nature is simply responding. Why do you think new earth must come forward? Because the *old* earth is polluted! Yet you *still* plug in! Don't you know that you can have electricity through the sun? But how many of you have done that and have acquired sovereignty in this area? *(Looks over silent audience and shakes his head)* Very few of you.

This Intensive is an Intensive on the days to come, but it is also one that poignantly tells you what you're not doing and how much you *don't* know.

If you are in harmony with Nature, you are *sovereign* with it. Then Nature will feed you. It will supply you with your electrical needs. It will supply you with your transport needs. It will build your hovels. And wherever you poke a hole in the ground, it will give you fresh water.

There are many things happening around your world that are being affected by Nature and being warred upon by it. Those things have been created by man. Nature is simply reacting for its life and its continuum.

I am sending you the runners—the ants, the knowingness of the sun, the trembling earth, and another runner, which is the awareness of where you live and what you have contributed to be in harmony with Nature. So be it.

Audience: So be it.

Ramtha: Now, there are those who have visions and who truly can see the shadows of today that create tomorrow. But what are the *attitudes* through which these entities describe their visions? Many ancient prophets who have seen the coming of cataclysms in Nature, have, through their own fears and limited beliefs, plagued many future generations as a result of their limited understanding.

I am teaching you this to bring you back into sovereignty so that you are not fearful, mindless, squabbling, defenseless people.

Why am I talking about this? So that you do not allow yourselves to become victims of the prophets. I am teaching you this to bring you back into sovereignty so that you are not fearful, mindless, squabbling, defenseless people. I love you. I teach you these things to engage you to be grander, to walk tall, to be in harmony, and to know.

The prophets are wrong about Nature and its *wonderful* life. They're wrong about the quaking and destruction and the infernal fires. It takes very, very little for a clever entity to upend all sound reasoning and have you give your power away to them.

To *know* . . . is to *do*. It is inherently within you to survive, even as lazy as you've become. "Why, the very thought of plowing the fields again and milking a cow! Really!" You need to be revived in spirit and in soul. That occurs when you come out of your illusions and become the sovereign entities that you truly are. If it takes planting your own food, do it. If it takes drilling your own well, do it! And if the drought never came, or if the earth never decided to do anything about herself, your sovereignty in Nature would allow the character of common sense to be cultivated in your direful social consciousness, the community of man. It would allow you to grow into your divinity.

Love of self is not a nine-to-five job. It is the harmonious movement of oneself in alignment with God, which is Nature. *That* is loving oneself.

These are *grand* times that are coming. They are birthing a new world, a new spirit, and a new understanding. The times that are at hand are Nature's march. So much so will she be on the march that very few entities are going to have time to think about war. They are going to be thinking about *survival*. That will build character and allow the humility to see the vanity of war and conquering and borders and mistrust.

Remember my asking you what are you are going to be

thinking about the moment the earthquakes occurs? That small manifestation, which *is* coming, is of a profound understanding that the *whole world* is getting ready to reason with. When that happens, what are they going to think about? Their political stands? Their nuclear weapons? Their mistrust, their hate, their bitternesses? Their coups, their power plays? They won't have *time* for that.

What has always deterred man from enacting grand madness? Divine intervention. What think you that is? Well, there was once a great and terrible wind that blew apart the Pope's armada, which was attempting to conquer England. What was it that destroyed the ships and the war machines? It wasn't *man*; it was Nature! That is "divine intervention." That's what will save this plane, and that is wonderful!

When you understand this, simply, and live in harmony with Nature, you will be the survivors in the new age that you are embarking upon.

I *love* you, but I see how unprepared you are for *everything*, because you've been looking in directions that can do no thing for you. I see the desire to know, but unless you are prepared, you are not going to survive. If you stay on your zippers, you are going to move, I assure you, and your homes will become rubble. Grand waves *are* coming. If you continue to live on the sea, your homes will be gone (and, perhaps, you also). Though you may think that this teaching is a lark, when the sun begins to spot itself and change, who are you going to borrow a biscuit from? Those of you who are insistent upon living in a city because it is close to work, ask yourself if it is worth it.

When the sun begins to spot itself, who are you going to borrow a biscuit from?

You are God. *(Shouts)* You are God! And you say, "Big deal. How is it going to change my job? How is it going to up my salary? How is it going to secure my mortgage? How is it going to help my relationship?" This that you are learning about is called Life. All of these other things have to surrender to this knowledge. If they don't, there is no life to wonder about. That is how it is.

The prophets did you a grave injustice, which you *allowed*

The prophets did you a grave injustice, which you allowed to be perpetrated upon you. You allowed yourselves to be a people of fear.

to be perpetrated upon you. You allowed yourselves to be a people of fear. You have taken for granted what really *is* spiritual, which happens to be life and everything in it, with Nature being the *Mother* that allows it to be.

This that you learn, *do* something with it! The change in Nature is already happening. You cannot sit on your haunches and say, "Well, she is going to take care of me because I've always liked her." That is ludicrous! Take the knowingness and the knowledge, and *feel what you feel*, and *move* according to that emotion. It will take you where you need to go. The god within you will take you in flow with this understanding. The change has everything to do with you—how you learn, what you feel, and what you do.

Now, contrary to popular belief, there are no UFO's coming to bag you up. It would be an *immense* babysitting job. I have heard that rumor, haven't you? Entities think that if they stand in a certain place and connect with their "higher brothers," they are going to come and get them and save them from all of this. Wrongo in the Congo.

You *do* have brothers who are in the seen and the unseen. That is a grand truth. Among them, you have those who are very intelligent, who have conquered gravity and have divine aeroships. They come here from many different galaxies. That is all true, true, true! But for some reason, you fantasize that they are going come and save you. That is not a grand knowingness; that is a limited fantasy. What is happening here is *your* destiny; it is *your* dream. They are also God, and they have learned to *allow*. In other words, you've made your bed, so they'll let you sleep in it—because obviously you *wanted* it this way! They're allowing you to realize *your potential*. That is *love*. And you *are* loved by them.

Nature is everything. There is nothing terrible about it; it is wholly sublime. Its evolution has brought you a *myriad* of beautiful things. Yet you have shaved down the forests of the earth for lumber, and you have done very little to put them back. You have taken from the natural elements. You have killed for gold. Nature has offered you everything that is sublime, but now it is on the move. This Intensive is the beginning of knowingness that will manifest throughout the end of this calender year. It is a *full spectrum* of understanding. If you do not know this, understand it, and embrace and love it for what it is, everything else that I have taught you in these audiences will have little meaning. Get it? So be it.

Nature has offered you everything sublime, but now it is on the move.

Audience: So be it.

Ramtha: I love you. You are learning. Your knowingness has been grand at this session. There are many who have embraced it, who have gotten it. It is the hour for you to rest. Take a reprieve from this audience for half your hour, then return. There are many things you need to do.

Refresh yourselves. Drink your water, heartily. Indeed?

Audience: Indeed!

Ramtha: I shall see you in only a half of an hour. So be it.

***

Saturday Afternoon Session
May 17, 1986

Audience members stream back into the hall. Ramtha remains seated until everyone is settled, then he rises to greet them.

Ramtha: You are refreshed?

Audience: Yes.

Ramtha: Well, you cannot gain wisdom if you are hungry, tired, or uncomfortable where you sit.

Now, know you that everyone has their own truth? For everyone is their own god; thus they have the power to determine their own reality. And whatever they determine reality to be, for them, they are correct.

So, in here, we have a most august body of gods. And it is wondrous to watch you, beloved entities, and see how you take the knowingness I have given you, filter it, and interpret it to create your own truth.

It is wondrous to see how you take the knowingness, filter it, and interpret it to create your own truth.

Now, change in the days to come. There are many things to come which involve the *natural* evolution of your wondrous earth and, indeed, of your solar system. I will give you a "wrap-up," if you will, on the evolvement of Nature, the wonderful Mother.

I watched your minds work. When I gave you the teaching concerning your Pacific Rim, your "western gate"—Mexico, the state of California, and part of the state of Oregon—I watched you understand and visualize that effect. Now I am going to reteach you regarding that understanding.

When I said your earth is moving north, into many of you

came the understanding that Mexico and California are becoming bedfellows with Washington and Canada. How you perceived what I said is that very shortly, those lands are just going to pick themselves up and mosey on along to the north. *(Audience laughs.)* See how you think?

What I *said* is, the plates are moving in a northerly direction in magnetic alignment. As a result, they are moving where the zipper flows— from deep into the equator, to Mexico, all the way up past Oregon, then taking a shift into the Pacific Ocean, meeting the Alaskan Gulf, and going on upward. What I am telling you is, the land mass—through plate tectonics and the earthquakes that come from pressure, and the volcanoes that are letting off the steam—is moving *very slowly*, so slowly that in your lifetime you shall never *see* Mexico become Oregon. But it *is* in movement, and it is going north, and that energy is creating land changes. Understand? *(Audience nods.)*

It is in movement, and it is going north, and that energy is creating land changes.

You are going to see more earthquakes this year. They will seemingly take rest in the year called '87 because much of the movement is already underway, and by then the pressure will have been relieved substantially.

When we talk of the quaking of the earth, one has to understand the *reason* it is quaking. There are different quakes. There is the rumbling underneath the great mountains that are fixing to vent their pressure. They are called volcanoes, mountains of fire. Then there are those quakes upon the zipper line where there are no mountains of fire. There, the pressure builds up to its greatest point.

You are going to have earthquakes along your Pacific Rim for the rest of this year. They will extend from the North American continent to the South American continent, all the way past your equator line. The greatest of these quakes shan't happen on the shoreline, but will happen along the fault line, the zipper, underneath the Pacific Ocean *near* the plate tectonic revolution. That *will* be felt in your country. But the greatest effect that will come from these quakes are the waves of water that will burst along your shorelines. The southern parts of Mexico, the lower part of California to the northern part of California, and southern Oregon will all feel the waves from these quakes. That is water coming. Know you what a wall of water looks like? That is when your view becomes *grand* if you are living there.

Those who live on the zipper are going to suffer the greatest devastation.

Those who live on the zipper are going to suffer the greatest devastation. And it isn't that they *should* suffer; they have simply chosen that for themselves, *knowing full-well where they are living*.

Now, changes in the earth's land mass. There is a new land mass that is creating itself at the present moment off the country called Japan, the Land of the Rising Sun. Grand name! It is a new shelf rising to the surface. The pressure of that shelf coming to the surface will create quite a bit of earthquake activity in Japan. That will end towards the latter part of '87. But they will begin to feel the rumblings very shortly.

When something rises, something must move to make room for it. Japan is going to be moving to the west to allow that which is arising on the east to be its closest neighbor. Toward the end of your century in counting, the people of the Land of the Rising Sun will only have to cross a small waterway to go into this new country. And they *need* it; it is a *blessing* to them. Upon that land, they will be able to cultivate and harvest foodstuffs that are liken unto the whole of the world's foodstuffs, for they will be able to grow anything and everything there. So rich and fertile will the land be, that it will allow them to be sovereign and self-sustaining. And that, indeed, is a blessing, and is well worth the trembling and the quaking that will occur in creating it.

As to Mexico, I would advise you, strongly, as one who loves you, to curtail your little visits there, beginning in your summertime and holding steadfast to that until the end of the year that is to come.

In your country, you are going to see mountains begin to arise where once there was nothing but a barren plain. The earth will rise due to the pressure from water flowing underneath it. That is a wondrous thing, for whenever a moun-

This is the Good Earth, the divine principle, taking things in hand and making changes, without asking you, in order to continue the process called Life.

tain arises, so do the plants, which add to the glory of what is *much* needed here, oxygen. This is *Nature*, your Mother, the Good Earth, the *divine* principle, taking things in hand and making changes—without asking *you*—in order to continue the process called Life. And if by chance your little farm is sitting in a wondrous little meadow, and you begin to find yourself ascending, be exceedingly glad.

Your underground nuclear tests are implosions, correct? The implosions that have been utilized by your country, not to mention other countries, have created a shock-wave effect in the solidity of your earth's crust. Where those implosions have taken place, the solid crust has splintered. As a result, you are standing on *shaky* ground because Nature *will* fill it back up. There is where mountains will start to form.

You are sitting within the borders of a grand country, for it is a country that is the housing of libertarian entities. Know you what libertarian is? Freedom of spirit! Freedom to change, to do as one wills to do within his capacity to *allow* himself to do that. In this country, you shall experience *much* of what Nature is doing. But the people of Europa and the Holy East and the Country of the Bear are going to be even more hard-pressed in the days to come. They have polluted their land, which feeds and nourishes them. They have polluted their water and their forests. Their fish are dying, their earth is poisoned, and that which eats from the earth is becoming poisoned. Not only have they polluted these things, but they are an unsettled, enslaved people who are endeavoring to outlive their enslavement by other nations and by rulers, creeds, doctrines and philosophies. They will not only experience a harrowing northern wind, but will also find it arduous even to sustain themselves in these days to come. Theirs, indeed, is a bleak plight.

Nature, in these ancient, ancient lands, is splitting the land masses apart, and they are moving northwest. This is creating earthquakes. The Ukraine, home to the children of the Bear, has a *splintered* core which needs to be filled up; and in the filling up process, earthquakes will be born. This ancient kingdom shall not only begin to move, but it is becoming a *dying* land, a *dying* place for the generations to come. In that process, there will be many earth changes throughout this decade and the end of the decade to come. Change on a mammoth scale, which would have taken 10 million years of evolution, will occur in only a single decade.

All of this is aggravated by man's desire for freedom. It is aggravated by minds that are suspicious of one another and filled with hatred for one another. It is aggravated by places that are ruled by heads of state whose own attitude has become political law, to which they subject their people. The people are "subjects of the crown," if you will.

In Europa, not only is the earth's crust moving west and then north, but other events are just beginning there. Plagues liken unto the Black Plague are now returning. They are plagues of diseasements but also of dire famine.

Nature, in its desire to clean up, make anew, and extend its surface ground and its living self, must go through many things. It would behoove you who are meek in your knowingness not to travel abroad. It would behoove you not to go outside the borders of your country. For this country and the people here have *the ability to change*. Understand?

It would behoove you not to go outside the borders of your country. For this country and the people here have the ability to change.

Audience: Yes.

Ramtha: Now, the people of the Land of the Bear, Europa, and the Holy East are *all* God. They are loved with the same love that is given to you and felt by you. Their plight is not without hope. Nature will refurbish itself and make itself anew. But that which *man* creates works in contention with Nature. Thus the manifestations that are occurring there are arduous and odious, indeed. It is not that these people are without help, for they are *loved*. But many things will come of the events that only now are coming to revelation, that are coming, poignantly, to *all* of the people of the earth.

Many of your countries devise, through fission, what is called nuclear energy. Know you what nuclear energy means? The energy in the nucleus of the atom. It is all-powerful but *raw* and still primitive. The reactors sitting around your world are susceptible to Nature. Because of underground experiments and implosions, the earth's crust has been fractured and splintered. And the earth, endeavoring to make itself anew, is going to shake and to create rumblings that will splinter your reactors. Entities, *you are in peril of your own doing*.

Now, I will allow Nature to stand for a moment, and I will go into the days to come of *man*.

You have come to my audience and have heard me speak to you a most *blasphemous* thing, a most *arrogant* and *selfish* thing—that you are God. You are God! And with that infinite, omnipresent understanding, you are *all there is*. And you hear, but nothing happens. You hear it, but you don't *know it*. It hasn't sunk in.

(Softly and deliberately) I came to you with the greatest message of all: you are God. Its simplicity has never changed. I have taught you this simple message again and again and again. It is in all the words I say to you in all of the audiences in my sojourn with you in this experience.

I came to teach, to *allow*, to circumvent the destruction of one's self, to manifest the runners to teach you things, to put you through experiences—all for the purpose of bringing a great entity forward. All of the runners and the experiences have been purposeful, because how do you know that what I say to you is a truth until you experience it. And I have not been above or below manifesting *anything* that would cause you to create knowledge and wisdom from it. But you *still* don't understand, and you are still hanging there.

Many of you still think God is outside of you. As long as you create God to be *outside* of you, you are disconnected from that which is *inside* of you. God is *not* an image. It is not separate from anything. God is everything. It is life, it is power, it is the moment. It is thought *realized* to become light. You *are* that wonderful light spectrum that was born when God, the Is, contemplated Self. Each fragment of light created from that contemplation held within it all of eternity—and that is *you*.

You say, "I certainly never thought God looked anything

like *me*.'' But being God has nothing to do with *looks*; it has everything to do with *attitude* and *knowingness*. It is the *essence* of one's character. It is the *power* of one's sovereignty.

Being God has nothing to do with looks; it has everything to do with attitude. It is the essence of one's character. It is the power of one's sovereignty.

How do you know that you are God? Because everything you are this moment, everything you do, everything you experience, has all been manifested by you—through *your* thought processes. In other words, you are having everything your way—because you *want* it that way! *Want* is the divine, wild, free will that has been your modus operandi for the ten million years you have been experiencing this plane.

Someone could say to you, ''Entity, is it not the grandest of days?'' and you could close your eyes and say, ''Alas, I see only darkness.'' You see how *powerful* you are? You have the power to shut out the sun. You have the power to embrace someone with love, or hold it back and have them suffer.

If you think that there is someone, somewhere in the unseen, pulling your strings, *dream on*, because there isn't! Only a god has the power to limit himself. Get it?

If you aren't happy, it's because you *want* to be unhappy. If you are sick, you *wanted* to be sick. You say, ''But I didn't really *want* to be this way!'' You *did*, because you have the *power* to change it *any moment* you *want* to. *Your* reality exists on *your* terms.

How do you, tenuous, limited entities, know that God is you—you who feel pain from your arthritic condition, heat in your loins, hunger in your belly, misery in your relationships, despise of yourself, hatred of other people? Because only a god can *feel* all those things.

Whatever you feel, you are *allowing* to occur through your thought processes. Know you that you would not be alive without the premise of Thought? Thought is God, and it feeds you. But you've been very clever, because you've blocked out two-thirds of your brain, and you've limited your ability to receive thought. And the more limited you are in thought, the more *direful* your life becomes.

How do you know you're limited? Think of all the things you think you can't answer for yourself (even though you can). Think of all the questions you have. Think of all the manic depression you have suffered. Think of all your unhappy moments. Think of all your floundering relationships. And when you can't take care of yourself, you are not only limited, you are *below* survival.

How do I teach you of something lost in your memory, something that does not fit into your schedules, your philosophies, your religions, or your family situations? I don't. All I am is a mirror to the possibilities that *all* of you will inevitably own up to. I mirror you back to yourself. But I can only mirror to you the knowledge of who you are. *You* must embrace it and apply it so that it will bring you to that feeling that *only you* can experience, embrace, and know.

I'll manifest for you. I'll send you the runners. All that I say will come true for the glory of God in all of you. One morning you will wake up and realize that these things have held witness to what I am teaching you. Then you will have the knowingness that you are indeed divine, that you create your own reality, that you are responsible for everything in your life. Without that knowingness, you shan't ever live to see and be a part of Superconsciousness, the New Kingdom, the New Jerusalem, a new time. You won't see it.

So, I tell you, in your simplistic, common speech, that you all created the pickle that you're in. All of you! You say, "How could I have been a part of the reactor accident at Chernobyl?" You have pity for the poor entities who are suffering there, but you think you didn't have anything to do with that because it happened in another country. The truth is, masters, you had *everything* to do with it, because you have not *allowed* your mind to wake up and become inventive and sovereign. Your political governments still have to rely on raw energy that is perilous to the human cell in order to keep you plugged in. Get it? Own it, because it is a great truth.

Where are your windmills?
Where are your solar energy systems?
You think you are enlightened,
but where, god,
is your sovereignty?

Where are your windmills? *Where* are your solar energy systems? You think you are enlightened, but *where* is your mind? *Where* is your motivation? *Where*, god, is your *sovereignty*?

You have added to your world's energy problems. And you will add to all of its other problems unless you create the attitude to change how you live, to manifest wisdom into action. Whatever you do is based on what you think; and whatever you are thinking is being fed back into the consciousness that feeds the thinking of everyone all over your world. It only takes *one* entity to start establishing *self-ordained* sovereignty. The feeling of that freedom, that allows one to sleep restful nights, goes out into social consciousness for someone else to pick up. That is how you become a "living the light to the world."

You will never *know* or discover who you are until you own up to your responsibilty in the events that are coming to pass. Only when you look at it and *own* it are you humble enough to change it.

Everything you have ever thought and embraced emotionally in your soul has manifested. Your thoughts, collectively, create your destiny. If you think that your purpose in coming here was to enact the "will of God," or because you are *supposed* to do this or that, that is *limitation*; that is one who is caught up in the social consciousness of reincarnation. A sovereign god, one who has found freedom in his own sovereignty, knows that he manifests his own destiny and that he can change it *this moment*, simply because he *wants* to.

You are *hypocrites* if you say on one hand that you have free will, yet on the other hand you worship and embrace preordained destiny. Think about it! No wonder you're limited. You've given away your power to the belief that you cannot change. You have cloistered yourselves in your closed minds and have become base survival entities rather than illuminated ones.

You've given away your power to the belief that you cannot change.

You think this is the Age of Aquarius? Bah humbug! The New Age? No, you're just old entities in a new body, in a new time, and you haven't really progressed anywhere.

Do you know that it took only a few sovereign entities to invent the freedom of being *mobile*. Do you know that you can count the number of inventors who created your Industrial

Revolution on both hands and have a few fingers left over. What did the rest of you do? You hopped on the bandwagon. You could not add your genius because you had not learned to be sovereign, because you think you are preordained, destined people. You say that you *are* sovereign? Only when you can supply all of your needs through your own endeavors are you a sovereign entity. Only then.

In his collective thinking, man has hardened himself against himself. He has lost the vision of his illuminated, divine personage. He has become a surviving entity who lives in the "slings and arrows" of incidence.

In my time, your earth plane was very different than it looks now. There were no oceans then. There was condensation of fresh water, but there were no oceans. Where your great America is, there was a great swampland with great land masses on either side. Because man had lost the vision of his illuminated self and had become a decadent, limited entity, lands where gods once walked in illuminated glory now lie beneath the sea.

Nature, responding to man's disrespect to his divine inheritance, endeavors to cover up his footprints and create anew. If the earth did not regenerate itself through change, man would become an extinct species, because the earth's stratum, which lives in a very delicate balance, is severely polluted. Even at the turn of your century, your people were choking from soot in the air. But the earth has and always will regenerate itself, and be glad for that.

You have created quite a pickle for yourselves.

You have created quite a pickle for yourselves. You cannot live together in harmony. You have many people who are your spoken and unspoken enemies. You are suspicious of entities whose color of skin is different from yours, and you consider many of them to be subhuman entities. You have divided your continents with boundaries and nations; and wherever there are nations, there are rulers; and wherever there are rulers, there is the clashing of specific attitudes.

The human race has been working up to an explosive state. Nations are vying to be the ultimate power, the ultimate ruler, controller, government. You have a great conflicts between religion and government. You have a great conflicts for allegiance. You have separated yourselves from your brothers, and, as a result, you have to post guards and create arms to protect your borders, your homes, and your children.

Know you war? You *should*; you do it *every day*. You do it whenever you argue your truth with someone else and tell them that they're wrong and you're right. That, indeed, is *war*. War doesn't have to be on a battlefield; it can be in your own backyard or in your own bathroom.

War doesn't have to be on a battlefield; it can be in your own backyard or in your own bathroom.

There is that which is termed "divine intervention" occurring upon this plane, because what has been created here is the threat of annihilation. Why do you think your rockets are falling from the heavens? You think they are simply malfunctions? Why do you think that your surveillance systems are being destroyed? Because your country, the Country of the Bear, and other countries are not up in space for scientific reasons. They are there to thrust themselves like eagles and make their nests among the stars in order to have dominion over heaven and earth. That is the desire of the warlords who lead your country and all other countries, no matter how small or meager they may be. After all, one who could sit at the pinnacle of a sunrise, who could hang on the silvery moon, would certainly have dominion over the rest of you. Because if that were to happen, what would you do? Spit at him?

Your attitude of pushing your philosophies, theories, and governments on other entities is coming to a close. That is much needed after seven and one-half million years of giving away your power and then struggling to get it back. In the days to come, the warlords who have desired to rule, who have been manifesting and fulfilling their dreams (because they too are gods), *are* going to rule; they are in the process of ruling. Those who sit abroad in the seats of government are dangerous, indeed, and they despise who you are. Though they are coming forward, it is like a sore that comes to a head and then bursts and oozes its vileness so that it can be healed again and made new. They are going to drop like flies because they are at the pit of their anger and their savagery, and they are losing their common sense mind. Their days are numbered, indeed.

The revolutions I have prophesied are all here. They are happening all over your world because the meek, the common people, are desiring and wanting only one thing to be theirs forever—the freedom to flow and ebb with life. The entities who are rising up to repress them will be brought down.

The greatest ruler any of you can have is that which is within you, that divine spirit which I am endeavoring to teach you about.

No bombs are ever going to destroy your country or the Country of the Bear. That will never happen. The forward movement of Nature is bringing an alignment, called divine mind, and that which is not in harmony with life will be no more. There are entities of renown, prestige, power, and pull, who will be ravaged by their own insidious selves and the attack upon them by others who are vying for their positions. It is an *individual* war for power. But these entities will fall in their tracks in front of you. By the end of 1987, few of these heads of state—or even their successors—will be left on this plane, for the time is over for those who breed the annihilation of the people of this plane.

The time is over for those who breed the annihilation of the people of this plane.

How do *you* add to all of this? By dividing yourselves. By thinking everyone is your enemy, when your real enemy is your *own perception*. The truth is, the people of the Country of the Bear and the people who are yellow in their skin—beneath each one's face and exterior lies someone *just like you*. Did you know that? They are the *same as you*. They are living gods, and it is *their* hour that approaches.

This nuclear accident at Chernobyl, know you the purposeful grandness of it? It was a little spark that will bring the land back to the people who plow up the potatoes, who bring in their own nourishment. This little spark will create a revolution in that great country. It shan't be one liken unto the Bolshevik Revolution. It shall be the meek inheriting their right to live in everlasting peace. Before the end of your next decade to come, the warlords of that country will have long passed this plane. This will leave open a grand spectrum of opportunity for the simple people there to recreate life, and *that* is a wondrous thing.

Your country is a biggie, eh? It is a grand place. It is the melting pot of the world. You are where people of all countries fled to find a new life. Your country is the representative of everyone in the world. *That* is magnificent. That stands for a unity of self.

You will not know war in this country, not on a cataclysmic scale. But you are going to learn to know yourself through Nature and its changes. And you will learn what it is to be God in its most sovereign sense.

You will learn what it is to be God in its most sovereign sense.

Now, many of you gripe and complain about your government not taking enough care of you. But what about *you*? Where is your sovereignty, enlightened masters?

Many of you complain about your King Reagan. But this entity is a *basic common-sense doer*, and he is ''on line''; he is right with the unfolding that is occurring. He is the first of three who will help create in this land the opportunity to return to a republic like the one envisioned by Solon, a government in which the people *rule themselves*. This movement in your country is *on schedule*.

Now, I did not vote for your king. But this entity *is* divinely inspired. It may not seem that way, but *every day* in his time the entity prays fervently for knowingness and direction. You don't know it, but I do. And it is from this outrageous, simple man that there will come into effect, before the end of your decade to come, a republic that has no head of state, one that is *ruled by its people*, a *great* republic, indeed. *(Audience applauds.)*

Many think they are being ruled by that now. You are not. You are allowing yourselves to be ruled by politicians. And that is all right. There are many of them who are noble in their virtue, and they are your brothers. But in Solon's republic, every entity was his *own* sovereign lord, and each took his allotted turn helping the country make decisions.

Why is that important for your country? Because your country was created to allow the destiny of freedom to come forward, and that freedom must be *absolute*; it must be complete in one's kingdom, and so it will manifest here. Your king, in spite of many things, is noble within his being. He has had the courage to be outrageous and different enough to make a difference for the common people; and so, such a republic will come to pass.

In the days to come, you will see many changes in your systems, your government, and your thinking. Each is a rung on the ladder to the freedom of the people. The warlords are dying; their thunder is being taken away. And what is coming to the surface, day by day, moment by moment, are *meek people* who, in the sincerity of their beings, have found peace with the whole of the world.

I desire for you to know that if all the common people of your world could speak their piece without the influence of their political doctrines, you would indeed find them charming. Then the barriers would be broken down.

Your government will sustain. It is on the wheel that will take it to the grandest freedom of all.

Your government, though it has been slandered and persecuted, even by those who are in it, *will* sustain. It is on the wheel that will take it to the grandest freedom of all. Those who live to see that hour will find joy and a freedom in their souls that will lift *all* consciousness to that understanding.

The entities who are rebelling are doing so to attain freedom in their lives. Did you know that? Know you who hates you? Those who desire to control their own people. To them, you are an unwanted reminder of what they don't want to occur in *their* country. Get it?

Audience: Yes.

Ramtha: So, collectively, the meek all over the world are casting the shadow of the days to come, of a grander world, a loving one that God certainly is the manifesting force behind. That is wonderful, and that is the shadow of what is coming.

There are many of you who shall never see that day when it breaks. Why? Look at what you are doing. Look at how you are living. You nod your heads and smile about the brotherhood of all people everywhere. You talk about loving all people, but *do you*? Do you love your neighbor? Do you love your family, without terms? What are *you* doing with *you*? Whatever it is, that is *your* destiny. If you drape yourself in the arrogance of intellectual pursuits, which entirely divides you against one of a simpler mind, you are not going to see Superconsciousness.

The lot of you individual gods need to look at what you are doing and how it is creating your tomorrow. I see you judge entities unmercifully. I have not found your love toward others warm and inspiring. You are selfish, indignant, arrogant, dying people. *Meek* you aren't! If you don't embrace who you are, the god that you are, and have the encounter called love, you are not going to see the days to come.

This is my teaching to you: Everyone you have judged for the two days prior to coming to this audience I am going to send back to you. So be it! *Every one* of them! Am I being cruel? Not at all. I want you to find the god within them, because you *need* to. When you do, you will have touched it within yourself, because you can see in yourself only what you see in others. All of those you have criticized are only reflections of you. The only way that you will truly know that you are humble and meek and everlasting is when you have seen those virtues in others. Do you understand?

Audience: Yes.

Ramtha: Allow others their truth. Know your own truth, yet be humble and meek enough to allow them to express their points of view.

Now, when you think of love, what usually comes to mind? Copulation and making out! Soulmates and marriage! You don't know how to love beyond those points of limitation. But true love is not physically inflicting affection upon another! It is getting down to what an entity is underneath it all, and *embracing* that divinity.

I'm going to send to you, my beloved brothers, entities who reflect every facet of yourselves, and the interlude will be both sweet and bitter. So be it.

When you love another, you are loving the mirror that allows you an insight into the truth of who you are beyond your morbid confusion.

When you love another, you are loving the mirror that allows you an insight into the simplicity behind your complexities, an insight into the truth of who you are beyond your morbid confusion. That is the wondrous thing you have been looking for since you forgot who you were, seven and one-half million years ago. Bless every runner from the lord-god of your being, because they are allowing *you* to know *you*. For every runner that you meet, ask yourself what facet of yourself the entity reflects and how you felt about that.

Love comes when you have loved yourself into joy. Joy allows you the sweetness to love the *whole* of the world, however they are. That is unconditional love; that *is* the crowning of a christ awakening.

If you wish to change, if you wish to be part of the changes that are coming about, you must learn to be humble in spirit. Now, what can we think of that can bring humbling of spirit? Hmm? *(Audience laughs nervously in anticipation.)* Bring 'em on! So be it!

Audience: So be it.

Ramtha: To be meek is to eat humble pie for a while. It is looking at someone you have hated, realizing that you didn't *see* far enough, and then being humble enough to embrace them. Humble pie is having told someone off and put him in his proper place, only to find out that you were in *gross* error (as usual when it comes to dealing with your brothers). Being humble is asking forgiveness of yourself for judging yourself. Being humble is taking a moment to listen to others and allowing them to be—no matter *how* their *being* grinds on you. That is being humble.

Be humble enough to forgive yourself. You can *never* ask anyone else to forgive you. They never do because they always remember; the memory is locked in their souls. You must forgive *yourself*. Speak from the lord-god of your being and forgive yourself—not for what you've *done*, but for *not knowing the god that you are*. Forgiveness is like a grand eraser. Know you a grand eraser on papyrus when you "oops"? Forgiveness takes away the guilt, the lowly spirits, the anger, the manic depression, and it allows you to feel like new wine. To be humble is to admit that *now* is the hour to know who you are and to go about things in a different way. That is being the meekest of all meek.

I am sending you a runner, *another* one. It is a vision of yourself. The vision you will see is one who has come to terms with himself and his god within, one who has learned what it means to be a god with unconditional love. I'll let you see a glimmer of what you can be. All of you in this room will have that vision before the summer is finished on this land. So be it!

Audience: So be it.

Ramtha: I look at all of you and I see the problems you create. Know you what a problem is? Ignoring the solution. I know of your complexities and your insecurities. I know of your fervent attempts at success. I know of your setting yourselves up for failure. I know of all the relationships that have gone awry. I know about *all* of them!

I look at you and I see your desperate need for advice. But before this year is complete, from what I will manifest, you will learn to embrace and understand your own reality and to change it. It does you no good to continuously seek outside of yourself for that which you already own within you. You are giving your power away if you do. Why don't you *know* the answers to your own questions? Why do you even *have* a question? You should just know it! Do you understand?

Audience: Yes.

Ramtha: It is not my desire to have you mimic an uncertain truth. It is my desire, as one brother to another, to manifest for you the wisdom for you to know with certainty, because you will never achieve change until you know the answer *by* yourself and *for* yourself.

You will never achieve change until you know the answer by yourself and for yourself.

If you want to know and to be powerful, you must listen to that grand voice within you. This voice doesn't say anything; it just *feels everything*. You are going to know what it is to touch an emotion that is divine and illuminated.

Now, I will show you how powerful I am—and how powerful *you* will become. You know all of your questions? I'll send you the answers. They'll be right in front of you. You are desiring to change relationships? I'll show you both sides of the coin. You are desiring success? I will exalt you, and in this year you will be successful. You are desiring to find joy? I'll send you a little joy. You are desiring to have peace so that you can sleep at night? I will send you nocturnal slumber. You are desiring an end to your woes, your hang-ups? I'll take you off the hanging-up and put you on a hang-down. So be it! You are happy?

Audience: Yes.

Ramtha: All that you came here to know, you will know. All that you need will be fulfilled. But know that this is done for the glory of God within you, which will stand as a witness to what is going to happen with you. And when they happen, know that *you* could have done these things all along.

Whatever the earth does, and whatever man does outside of your own small place in your world, really doesn't matter unless *you* are in control of what *you* do, and you know and understand who you are. So be it. I love you forever, and ever, and ever.

(Studies the audience) You are at a peak of absorption. You have absorbed grand things, and the lights are coming on. I am very pleased with you. Despite the size of this audience and the uncomfortableness that you may have endured in being here, you have learned grand things. You have embraced them in the spirit of a true master, one who embraces knowledge so that he is in control and has the ability to change. You have come a grand way in the consciousness that you have created through this audience.

There are no words in your common speech to tell you how much I love you. When this Intensive is finished, and we have gone through the rag-tag of events that are already coming—and those that you are going to change because you *want* to—there will be a sweet and delicious feeling inside that is more illuminated, more free, and more understanding.

You know, you are coming into energy *(points to the video*

cameras). Through your learning this day, you are going to be a light to all of the people of the world, because people, even in the Land of the Bear, are going to see this moment. Without that which you have come to in your understanding and your learning, it would never be made manifest. So, that speaks grandly of the quality of entities who are gathered here. I bless and love the *lot* of you.

Through your learning this day, you are going to be a light to all the people of the world.

I desire for you to go and manifest for yourselves a breath of fresh air, some foodstuffs (make it hearty), and a glass of crystal water. Then go and find a place, and sit down and contemplate. Just be alone with that which you are. You *need* to. For in that aloneness, grand things will occur that will have profound effects on your days to come. Indeed?

Audience: Indeed.

Ramtha: When the hour becomes five, come back to this audience. You will be ready to hear some more. So be it!

Audience: So be it!

Ramtha: That is all.

***

Saturday Evening Session
May 17, 1986

Ramtha, seated on stage, watches attendees as they fill the room. Once all members are seated, Ramtha stands, and the audience applauds and cheers.

Ramtha: Indeed! Wonderful *gods*, you are empowering everything! Well, I am pleased. *(Studies audience)* You are rested?

Audience: Yes.

Ramtha: Nourished?

Audience: Yes.

Ramtha: Contemplative?

Audience: Yes.

Ramtha: Very contemplative. You have been comparing . . . what is the term? . . . "notes." *(Audience and Ramtha laugh.)* Well, well, well. And *who* is really right, after all?

My beloved entities, most of you here have grasped a great deal with a joyful soul. Rather than looking toward your tomorrow with gloom, you are looking at it with anticipation. It is what you call "turning around." I am pleased. *(Picks up his glass and toasts)* To change!

Audience: To change!

Ramtha: To Life! Forever, and ever, and ever. So be it!

Audience: So be it!

Ramtha: There has been a saying in your social circles that history repeats itself. Well, there is only *one* creature in history that ever repeated itself in a *mire* of redundancy, and that is the humanoid entity, mankind.

There is only one creature in history that ever repeated itself in a mire of redundancy, and that is the humanoid entity.

Nature never repeats itself, for it is the continuum of evolution. But man is *certainly* getting a little boring. Lifetime after lifetime has been squandered by attitudes that are restrictive and without the nourishment of unconditional love, because those attitudes have been playing over and over again. So, in the drama of man, it does not matter what *time* in history it was. It does not matter what you wore then, how you got around, or the state of your technology. It was your *attitude* that mattered. For what you are this day—what you are thinking this day and embracing in emotion—you become in your tomorrow.

Man, in his collective social consciousness, has been a very awesome and destructive entity. He sets up his destruction in each life, only to return and feel it in the next lifetime. He sets up an attitude that creates the playpen for his children, who are the seeds of his return to this plane. But man is slowly waking up from a dream that has kept him on the wheel of life over and over and over again.

Contemplate your history for a moment and what you have learned about ancient times and ancient civilizations. How many times has a particular country risen to power, gone under, risen to power again, just to fall again? It has happened over and over and over. It is happening even this day in your time.

Change in the human attitude happens when an entity comes to the end of his rope and no longer desires to live the human drama. He desires to get off the wheel of life—the cycle of living, dying, and being reborn—and finish the dream of limitation, and it *is* a dream. Then he has *absolute* control of his life once again.

It is utterly up to you to create your destiny and the attitude of self-destiny.

In the days to come, it is utterly up to you to create your destiny and the attitude of self-destiny. This is important for the *whole* of mankind, in all places. You are approaching the time when this is going to be necessary for the survival of these entities who are gods asleep in the dream called mankind. In the days to come, the whole of all peoples need to reassess the seeds of their virtue. This is already beginning to happen.

What has always been a terrible trauma of the human drama are religions that teach of a judgmental God that is arduous to please, that dooms you if you do not follow strict regulations and orders. For eons, insidious dogmas have created war amongst all of the people of your world because of the prejudice toward one who believes in God differently than another. You think I'm talking about *primeval* man? Even this day there are ravishing revolutions and hideous, secret wars all over your planet—and they are called "*holy* wars."

What ever could be holy about warring against another's truth?

What ever, *ever*, could be holy about warring against another's truth?

Did you know that every war that has occurred throughout your history has been based on the clash of religious beliefs? on one group of entities pressing hard its laws and regulations upon another group, which had its own. Did you know that?

There is coming forward a great polarity and turbulence in regard to this, for man is beginning to wake up and realize that what is important is not to *believe* in God but to *embrace* God. Belief is tenuous, and it is without the power of manifestation.

There are no miracles in belief, only in *knowingness*. Your world is getting ready to encounter the decadence of holy wars in epic proportions, all to be fought "in the name of God." There will come an hour, my beloved masters, when a new consciousness and a new understanding will press hard against your awesome indifference. This new consciousness has nothing to do with dogma, rules and regulations, or ancient beliefs that have terrorized you in your dream. It has *everything* to do with personal sovereignty. You who all are gathered here, through the change you will manifest in the days to come, will make a grand difference on this plane. You are direfully needed.

The reason that history has repeated itself is that you have allowed God to be taken out of you. And in your search for God in outer perimeters, you lost sight of it in the inner perimeter. You allowed yourselves to become bastards of the universe, spawns of an uncertain God. You allowed your-

You gave your divinity away to others and you allowed their dogma to speak on the behalf of God.

selves to be anything other than divine. You freely gave away your divinity to some elusive power that sits way outside of you. You gave your divinity away to others and you allowed their dogma speak on the behalf of God.

What has kept you on the wheel of life? *Attitude*. What has kept you asleep in the dream? *Guilt*, the feeling that you are unworthy to see the face of God. Lifetime after lifetime, you have spun your wheels, you have warred and been warred against, and you have died of ravaging diseases—all because of your guilt! That hour is coming to a close. What you allowed to be taken away from you is coming back home.

I am teaching you to embrace the Father within. That is embracing *you*, the greatest temple there ever was, the garden within where the christ can be reached *in a moment*. That temple, that sacrament, that divinity, that illuminated self, which has *always* been there, is home. And that consciousness-understanding is pressing against the lot of you. Those who embrace themselves and the christ within are going to create a great polarity on this plane; and all who are warring in the name of God will enter into a great battle, which will then cease.

Mankind's pettiness of attitude, his bickering, his limited definition of God, are all coming to a close before the end of this decade. What has been raging in the Land of the Green will be finished. And what of the Jewish people and their wandering years, and their coming back to their proclaimed homeland? To create their own state was a wondrous thing, indeed, but what of the entities they kicked out? What about *their* beliefs? Where is *their* home? Where do *they* go? Is their God not connected with their soil and temples? To them, he is.

The understanding that God the Father, the divine scepter, is within every entity is coming to all people. Even those who are still warring to the last grain of sand for their holy land will be affected by this understanding before the end of this decade.

Light, understanding, knowledge—it raises you up from

the murk and the mire and lifts you above the warring hordes. It allows you to be at peace, wherever you are. But if you don't embrace this understanding, you will become the victims of a raging Nature in her evolutionary patterns.

The understanding that God is within everyone is being pressed to your plane. It is the hour of change for the human drama. It is the meek, the gentle entities, who will awaken mankind from his slumber. It is a knowingness that is without words, that is *wholly* energized of its own purity. Those who *believe* in God can never put forth a certainty. Those who *know* that the kingdom of heaven is within have touched the hand of God in a rejuvenation of spirit. That essence, that knowingness, that attitude of certainty isn't going to enslave religions, quite the contrary; it will bring reason and understanding to them. There are warlords and terrorists and revolutionaries who are spurred by the dogma of religion; *their* hour of change is also at hand.

The coming change of the human spirit will not take away the illumination of God; it will enhance it, by removing the laws, the threats, the urgencies, the fears, the intimidations, and all that has suppressed a wonderful people for *eons*. To be free is not only to cultivate the soil to rear up your own staff of wheat. It is not only having the sense to create your own "electrum." It is not only living as a sovereign, wholly. To be free is also to know that you always move in the grace and the love of the Father within you, the great Is, the great Allower. It is *knowing* that you are always loved, and that all of your experiences have been purposeful and needed in order to cultivate compassion and love for *every entity*.

How utterly free you will be when you know that you have never been judged by God.

How free, how *utterly* free you will be when you know that you have *never* been judged by God; that you have always been loved by the Father within you; that the christ is not only Yeshua ben Joseph [Jesus Christ] but is latent within *every* entity within the *whole* of the world! *That is the new understanding*.

Heresy, you say? Truth! You have been allowed to be limited and ignorant *because* you are loved. You think that

God would hard-press you? Never. You have done that yourselves.

Your becoming, your awakening, is certain. If you pass this plane, what awaits you on the other side of this life is *splendor*. To know that is to meet your hour of passing with grace, dignity and joy, rather than with sorrow, guilt, insecurity, and terror.

There is coming a knowingness to all people that the only one who has ever judged them has been their own selves and those who have judged them into submission for the purpose of control. How *grand* it will be for all people to know that regardless of the religion or creed they belong to (even if they don't think they belong to one, they do), when the dogmas are all melted down and removed, they will be free people. How grand it will be when the holy warriors realize that there is nothing to fight about "in the name of God"—that God never needed *fighting* for, God is *living for*. Get it?

Audience: Yes.

Ramtha: Change and the human drama has very much to do with one's concept of his own beliefs, his own worship, and how he goes about it. To the lot of you in this room, there is coming to each of you, individually, a redemption of the spirit of what God is. In that process, you are going to be rocked to the *root* of your beliefs, even those you thought you no longer had. You are going to test yourselves in your absolute knowingness of unconditional love, in your knowingness that God truly is within you. You are going to experience, face to face, the possibility of christhood. And the face? It will be your very own. All the runners to come are sacred and wonderful, because they will reflect back to you who you truly are. They are perhaps the greatest of all, because when you know *absolutely* who and what you are, then you are in *complete* freedom; then you are a meek entity that is in *complete* sovereignty.

You are going to experience, face to face, the possibility of christhood. And the face? It will be your very own.

In the days to come, before the end of this decade, holy wars will be at their zenith. But as quickly as they came to enslave people of this plane, they will cease. Only then will there be peace in the Holy East, in Europa, even in your country, where religions and creeds are vast and myriad, and are pulling and tugging at everyone from every direction to get them to repent. Repent for *what*? For *living*?

Religion and dogmas are coming to a close. What is coming forward is not collective truth but *individual* truth. Then sovereignty can be absolute. These are the days of the heralds of the peace of Superconsciousness. So be it. *(Picks up glass and toasts audience)* To the Father within. Forever, and ever, and ever. So be it!

Religion and dogmas are coming to a close. What is coming forward is not collective truth but individual truth. Then sovereignty can be absolute.

Audience: So be it!

Ramtha: Man is changing, but he is not leaving behind tradition altogether; rather, he is doing away with the *enslavement* to tradition. He is coming forward with a vital move and surge into a time that is joyous, that is jovial, that is exalting. It is what you term the upbeat side of the days to come.

After the runners and the visions and the embracing, it will still be up to you as to what and how much you want to do—or how much you want to *exasperate* yourselves. It still comes down to you. There are those of you who will go a grand distance, and there are those of you who will go a *short* distance. But know that throughout all of the changes that are coming forth—the earth moving and changing, the dying out of warlords, the rebirth of new principles, the rebirth of the dignity and rights of all people—individual destiny is being created in each moment according to your attitude and how you see the changes that are coming forth.

Many will perish in the days to come because they will not *change* their attitudes. They will not face, embrace, and erase their limited selves in order to do away with the dream that has kept them repeating themselves, lifetime after lifetime.

Now, there is no entity, no matter how grand, who can ever change your attitude *for* you. Your attitude is *your* "will of God." If you choose to hold on to things that are of no importance, and you do not prepare and take care of yourselves in the meekness of humility, you are going to perish in the days to come. And you must know you have chosen that destiny because you *wanted* it.

Man can avert every war, if he wants to. Man can meet every challenge, if he so desires. Man can embrace his brothers, no matter where they are, if he wants to. Man can be the peacemaker, if he wants to. Man can heal himself, if he wants to. Man can *live*, if he wants to.

The days that are coming are the days of black and white; there will be no gray. One will either be in the throes of change, creating right within himself, or he will die with the old and be remembered no more. That is how it is. These are not the days for those who walk the middle of the road. These are the days for those who are *doing*.

These are not the days for those who walk the middle of the road. These are the days for those who are doing.

There are many doers in this audience, and I am exceedingly pleased at that. Doers are manifesting gods. All they need is to *know how to know*, and they will do. And there are those of you here who cannot let go of your beliefs, dogmas, bigotries, predjudices, insecurities, and guilts. You will not see Superconsciousness, because you have not humbled your pride to allow yourselves to see it. And that is all right. Death is not an ominous thing. Choosing whatever you want to do is your right. But know that you are choosing, and take full responsibility for that. You are loved *regardless* of what you do. You have *always* been loved regardless of what you do. You cannot fathom how well you have been taken care of to keep you from destroying yourselves.

It is a crucial moment of awakening. The attitudes of the people of the world are now in motion. The days to come, the birthing of these changes, lead to a new kingdom and a new understanding, a place that I call "Superconsciousness." But right at this moment, it is not only important that you listen, but that you *embrace* this new awakening emotionally, and that you have the courage to be humble enough to understand it. Nature will continue to move on in spite of you. *Your* territory for change is *your attitude*, and that is within your own dominion. And what you change affects the whole. That is how *you* make a difference. Whether you are going to go back to sleep or whether you are going to live and profoundly affect the *whole* of humanity is up to you. You understand?

Audience: Yes.

Ramtha: Now, you are called "new age" thinkers, eh? *(Ramtha and audience laugh.)* I'm happy you're thinking! Be at peace with what you are and with what you are doing and feeling. Understand that it is for the Father within you, and that you are in the process of waking up. Do not, I beseech you, be intimidated out of your knowingness. It will be *easy* for you to give it away again and go back to sleep when someone says, "You are *all* wrong!" You're *never* wrong when something *feels* right. Never!

Be a light to the whole of this world. Appreciate life. Learn to love everyone, for they *all* are the Father.

I love you. *(Picks up his glass of water and toasts audience)* To new age thinkers!

Audience: To new age thinkers.

Ramtha: I desire for you to feel and embrace what I just told you, and to "sleep on it." This teaching has been on what is called the freedom and the love of God for you. Knowing that, *unconditionally*, will heal many who are diseased in this room. It will heal those who are without joy. It will answer the questions. And it will bring forth a new understanding which all of you need. This teaching, and me nagging you this evening will produce a new tomorrow. So be it. That is all.

(Ramtha starts to leave, and a man shouts, "We love you!")

I am *worth* loving, entity! *(Laughs while audience applauds)* When you can say that to me, and feel it, then you have touched your *own* love and your own light. Because, after all, I am *just* a grand mirror. So be it. I'll see you in your dreams. That is all!

***

Sunday Morning Session
May 18, 1986

Ramtha, seated on the stage, observes attendees as they enter the hall. Once they have taken their seats, Ramtha looks them over warmly, steps down from the platform, and begins to mingle with them. He slowly works his way through the audience, stopping to touch and speak to individuals. The audience watches intently as Ramtha makes his way around the room.

Ramtha: (To a woman standing near the platform) I wish to help you and your family find your own joy and what life means to you. It will become very clear soon. *(Walks over to a man and places his hand on the man's shoulder)*

Man: (Whispering) I want to make sure I'm making the right move. And I want to know where I should be.

Ramtha: Don't you?

Man: (Shaking his head) No.

Ramtha: You *will.*

(Walks on and stops in front of an older woman sitting in a wheelchair) Know you that you have loved more by being in this chair than most have who can run amuck? One day, lady, you will walk away from this chair, I assure you. *(Kisses both sides of her hands)*

Woman: Thank you, thank you.

Ramtha: Just know.

(Walks over to a woman who is smiling) You have a beauteous face—because it laughs a lot. *(Audience laughs.)*

(Speaking to the entire audience) There will come an hour when all of you know how beautiful you truly are. You have yet to see that in yourselves. How could you. You wrap yourselves up in so many troubles and worries and expectations that are only illusions. *(Walks over to a young, pregnant woman)*

Woman: (Almost crying) Would you bless my child?

Ramtha: Indeed. *(Bends over, places his hands on the woman's abdomen and wordlessly blesses the unborn child)*

Woman: Thank you.

Ramtha: Take heart lady. The fruit of your womb is a grand entity, for all who are coming in now are great masters. What has plagued your generation and humanity will never plague this child—not disease, nor war, nor discrimination, nor misery. Your child will know what it is to be tranquil in spirit and humble in its divinity. So rejoice.

Woman: (Weeping) So be it.

Ramtha: And so it will be.

Beauty is not the skin; it is what issues forth from within.

(Addressing the audience) What is beauty? It is not the skin, it is what issues forth from within. All of the paint and color and your thinness will never make you beautiful. It is what you *are* that exudes beauty. One must take great care to ripen that spirit. Those who come to my audience will learn about such beauty. Many love me and think that I am beautiful, yet they have never seen my face. So it is with you. You have never *seen* yourself. One day you will. Then you will know what love I greatly about you.

(To a man standing by the wall) It does not matter who I am. What matters is gaining the understanding of who *you* are. That is indisputable. *That* you will learn. Indeed.

(Walks over to a white-haired lady) After you have been through all of the teachers, all of the guides, and all of the material, you will find that nobody knows better than you, that the truth was within you all along.

Woman: I think I'm becoming aware of that.

Ramtha: You are going to need to. So be it.

(To a young woman) I love you, lady. In the days to come,

you will find me around you and your wondrous children more than ever before.

Woman: I love you. *(They hug each other warmly, then Ramtha walks over to a man seated near the aisle.)*

Ramtha: Master, I desire for you to know how much I love you. I have watched you, and I have seen you run away from life. I have seen you frightened and insecure and, for the most part, wanting to listen but also not wanting to listen. I love you, and I always will. There will come an hour when you will arise in your morning and everything will be very clear. And all the illusions? They will have fallen away, and you will have fallen in love with what you are. And you shan't ever allow that love to be destroyed by you or anyone else. It matters not what you have done before; it is who and what you are *now* that matters. The past is rotting pages of papyrus that the wind will blow away. All that matters is the emotion and the wisdom that is left; that is the grandest treasure of all. Above all things, you must learn how beautiful you are. *(Filled with emotion, the man nods in agreement. Ramtha kisses his hands then walks to another man who has a very serious, concerned expression.)*

It matters not what you have done before; it is who and what you are now that matters.

Perhaps I seem very harsh in what I teach. But, master, I did not come here to win over converts or friends. I already am your friend. I love you.

Man: (Nods) I know.

Ramtha: It is often arduous to come to the simple understanding of self-created realities and what will flow in Nature in the days to come. It is difficult, I know, but this understanding is the basis and the premise to which we must inevitably return, naked in our understanding and in our surrender to it, and joyful in our experiences of our past, knowing that they have ripened us to embrace what we are completely. I love you, and always will.

Man: I love you and always will.

Ramtha: Stay happy.

(Ramtha by now has circled the entire hall and is back in front of the speaker's platform. He holds the hand of a vibrant

woman.) You have done great things for humanity. You have not seen it yet, but you have. It only takes one who knows with conviction. Lady, in the days to come I am going to be the wind at your back. And critics who have been belligerent in their judgment of you will be no more. Stay steadfast.

Woman: (Weeping tears of release and joy) I will. I will. I want to go where you are.

Ramtha: You are going to. Live in *great joy*, entity.

Woman: I shall.

Ramtha: (Takes the hand of the man sitting next to her) You can climb the highest peak. You can go into the deepest valley to seek the elusive master who knows all, guides all, and takes care of all. But no matter where you go and who you shall see, no matter if they are brilliant in their exposition and wise in their counsel, know that you will never find what you are seeking. For no one can give you the love and the wisdom and the impeccable life that you can give *you*. You have to go nowhere to find that. *(Kisses his hands)* You have to do nothing—no rudimentary exercises, no chants, no austere living—to contact that which you are. You only have to want to; then the path is indeed short. Love what you are. Do not limit its measure. Do not pit yourself against others and war with them. Do not measure your greatness by the deeds of others. There is no one greater than you and the Father within you—an impeccable christ. Understand?

Do not pit yourself against others and war with them. Do not measure your greatness by the deeds of others. There is no one greater than you and the Father within you.

Man: Yes.

Ramtha: Live your light so that it is brighter than the morning sun, so that your days are filled with warmth and beauty, and your valleys are alive with the busyness of life.

Man: So be it.

(Ramtha walks down the aisle and stops in front of a woman in a beautiful blue dress.)

Ramtha: Lady, when others have fled because they think I am controversial, you have stood your ground. What a grand lady you are. Hold tight. I have plans for you.

Woman: More plans?

Ramtha: Indeed, but *grander* ones.

(Turns to a beautiful young woman who gazes intently at Ramtha as he speaks to her) It takes, perhaps, a long time to let go. It often takes even longer to live your own truth in spite of social consciousness. When everyone is wanting you to do this or do that, it is very arduous to be sovereign, stand your ground, and still love them and allow them their truths. But you *can* exalt yourself into knowing and then *living* that knowingness.

You are persistent. You keep coming back because you haven't got it yet, but you're going to, entity. Little by little the understanding comes, the nobleness of spirit comes, and the strength to live compounds itself.

Little by little the understanding comes, the nobleness of spirit comes, and the strength to live compounds itself.

To contemplate leaving this plane is a travesty. To see the days to come in all of their glory and the change that will exalt this plane, you've got to *live*. I am pleased that you are endeavoring to become. I love you for that. So be it.

(Looks at a woman in the next row) Live by your conscience, not by what others say. Understand?

Woman: Yes.

Ramtha: Live by the *feeling*. *(Chuckles)* And don't lose yourself in it.

(To the entire audience) I love you. *(Climbs the stairs to the speaker's platform)* I love you. You are grander and more dear to me than you can fathom. Wherever you go upon this plane, and whatever you do, I will always be the wind that is around you. For those of you who take this truth and this knowingness into your souls, and release that which limits the grandness of your becoming, you will see the days to come. A grand wind will carry you there. You are my brothers. Once, you lived in my army.

You are the reason I have come back here for a sojourn. I am waiting for the hour for you to *know* who you are. In great repetition, I have taught you a *simple, simple* truth, waiting for you to wake up. You are the hope of the world. You don't know that, but you *are*.

Where is one who can embrace the whole of the world and love all people regardless of their faith, their political ideals,

When there's peace, there is joy; and when there is joy, there is God, remembered and embraced.

or their past? Where is one who can love them and *allow* them? In allowing, one nurtures, unequivocally, peace. When there's peace, there is joy; and when there is joy, there is God, remembered and embraced.

What would life be if what you have lived thus far was all there was to life? There *is* more. But you are *stagnated*, repeating yourselves, and not at all evolving like Nature is. There is much more to that brain of yours, which is only on one-third operational power. When you open to this understanding and embrace what you are, it will bring to the world its greatest hope and its greatest revelation.

(Looks tenderly at the audience) I love you. There is *grandness* in your beings. There is *illuminated* divinity there.

The days to come are *riddled* with changes that will affect you all. But far greater than what the future holds is where you are in your discovery of yourselves.

I love to walk with you. I love to be in your slumber. I love to look into your eyes, to touch your delicate hair and delicate skin, and connect with your souls. To me, though you are vast in numbers, you are unique and grand and God—that which love I, that which be I, that which see I in all of you. The purpose of this teaching is not only to prepare you for the days to come; it is to help you *ripen*, and to plant the seeds of discovery within yourselves. These days and the things that are at hand are only the backdrop of the stage upon which you are going to finish your act. When one by one you begin to wake up, and you realize and embrace and know what you are, then you are free, free as the wind.

This is not, as you term it, a "pep talk." It is the most profound truth of all. Your adventures in discovery have little to do with technology; they have everything to do with going within and discovering the unexplored regions of your identity. To do this, you must peel away, *one by one*, the limitations, the clouds, the layers of your limited identity—by *humbling* yourselves to do it—until you find the light that is within and hear the voice that speaks to you in tranquil, sublime emotion. It is God. When you have reached that, you have come home.

Many of you have doubted who be I. You have done so because it has eased your task of discovering who you are, since I remind you of who you are. That is all right. It does not hurt me, for I do not hurt; I only love. So it does not matter about me. In these days that are coming, it is *you* who must matter to *you*. I *know* who and what be I, which is everything. It is now time for you to know who *you* are.

When I asked you of your desires, knowing full-well what the result of them would be, I sanctioned the *lot* of them, because they were what you *wanted* to experience. Could I tell you, "Don't desire it."? You think a god would say that to you? Hardly! He would *allow* you. Because he knows that through experience and the wisdom thereof, you are going to wake up; you will *own* the experience of that desire and, indeed, that dream. You understand?

I have done many things for many entities; I have sanctioned all of their dreams. And yet, when they manifested, I was also blamed for all of their miseries. I'm a heavy! *(Audience laughs.)* In an uncomfortable awakening, when you begin to see that you are in charge of your reality and it comes home to you in *fiery* emotion, you want to close your eyes again and say, "I do not want to go forward! It is all your fault!"

I have challenged the lot of you gathered in this room. What I have spoken to you, 'tis an individual, indisputable truth that has moved within all of you. There will come an hour when it will burst forth completely. Then you will no longer blame or accuse anyone; you will embrace the whole of it and say, "I *made* it this way. *I* chose it." Understand? But now, you're like little children. If something doesn't work, you point fingers. If you fall down and hurt your knee, you cry out very loudly. But there is coming an hour when you are going to grow up and come to the other side of the dream. That is what I am waiting for.

You're like little children. If something doesn't work, you point fingers.

Now, I have many audiences coming forward. And you wonder, "Which one do I go to?" I did not create these audiences so that you need to go to every one of them! These audiences are wisdom given forth so that you may open up your eyes again and go home. There *is* coming the day when you will have awakened and owned it all, because you will have realized that you have created it all. You will have realized how *powerful* you are. Then, what else needs to be said? Hmm? I will have come and been a mirror to you. One day there will be no need for the mirror any longer. And what awaits is a vastness of unexplored life that is your kingdom of heaven. One by one, you'll come home to where be I—and *that* is an adventure in itself. Until that hour comes, I will be here to teach—not to be worshipped—and to challenge your closed minds to wake up. Whatever it takes, from the earth trembling to ants running amuck on your counter, I will do it, because you have desired it.

The greatest love is only between equals, and I'm your equal.

I love you. There can never be true love when there is a follower and a teacher. The greatest love, unconditional love, is only between equals, and I'm your equal. Your *equal*. Get it?

Audience: Yes.

Ramtha: You do not realize through what time barriers and dimensions this miracle has occurred. Though you take it for granted, contemplate the mastery and the ownership and the power that it has taken to be here with you, on common ground, utilizing your *outrageous* common speech. I have expedited your time in order to be with you, to walk with you, to talk with you, and to allow the feelings to come forward. That is a precious gift. I love you. So be it! *(Picks up his glass of water and toasts)* To Life. For Life, *as it is*, is the display of God, and it will live on, forever, and ever, and ever. So be it!

Audience: So be it!

Ramtha: Now, after listening to you and watching you think, I am going to clear up some misunderstandings. I did *not* say that earthquakes were going to rock the world and sink it. That was what one entity derived from my teaching. I *did* say that new earth will be coming forward.

To clarify: The ''ring of fire'' is *on* the Pacific Rim. The Pacific Rim refers to the lands that a zipper runs through and around.

Now, there is a long sinuous crack at the bottom of your Pacific Ocean. In its depths lies what is liken unto an inflamed sore, except this sore doesn't heal. This is a regenerating process of new land masses coming up from beneath the ocean floor. This process is creating new plates of earth, and they are moving to the east and the west. Above the equator, they are moving northeast and northwest.

From the new land mass that is coming forward, one day will be born new continents, new islands, new channels. Mexico and California are taking a stroll northward. *Every moment*, new plates are being issued forth in the Pacific Ocean. These plates are putting pressure on the zipper, and the pressure is causing the land mass to *inch* its way north in *subtle* movement.

There are areas where entities live upon the zipper. The attitudes of these entities are such that they are living a suicidal understanding. Know you what "suicidal understanding" is? They are the entities who are defying Nature. Their attitude is in a state of unharmonious life. This *intensifies* the energy around that particular zipper, and quickens and makes greater the devastation than would normally be, because they are manifesting gods who are affecting Nature. They are manifesting the means to their own end. That is their choice. They *want* to, and it is all right.

The attitudes of these entities are such that they are living a suicidal understanding.

Now, about the east coast. I heard an entity blatantly say, "But of course, you know, Florida is sinking." It *is*. It is allowing the Atlantic Ocean to *slowly* but *surely* go under its crust and come up within its land mass. That process, that has been going on for quite some time, *will continue*. Those who have made their hovels in this state or country, whatever you call it, are not in danger of drowning. But they have put themselves in a position where they face great suffering due to the fury of the storms that Nature is creating. That is their choice, and that is all right.

Now, regarding the poisonous water of the New England states, the water there is *treacherous*. Entities are drinking their own urine, their own waste. Because of the industrial movement therein, they are also poisoning the stratum. When the rains come, they are like a glass of myrtle: they are poisonous. The earth is so polluted in those areas that the rain is not filtered clean by the earth. Your forests and your fishes are being destroyed by the rain. Your industrial waste is killing off creatures that live in the salty waters of your oceans. That has been going on for some time. Those who live in the moment and take their chances and continue to manufacture, because it has seemed important that industry survive, are uncaring of the environment that supports them. There are changes coming, for I love the dappled woods and the elusive fish which appear liken unto a pearl when hit by the light of the sun. Prepare yourselves in the days to come for Nature's *re*action to those who live in those particular states.

Now, another thing that I heard in a conversation in an entity's room was in regard to the question, "Where to move?" Sound familar? *(Audience laughs.) Big* discussion—"Where to move?"

For a long time in your counting I have been advising entities to leave the Atlantic Seaboard and New England, and make a pilgrimage to the western sphere. That has been very purposeful. Many of them have rallied and have made their pilgrimages, and they have found themselves a rejuvenating life there.

Do not live in the cities.

If you cannot move from the Eastern Seaboard because you have found so *many* reasons why you cannot, this will be temporary relief until you embrace the whole of the knowingness I have given you: Stay, but do *not* live in the cities. *Do not live in the cities*. For in the days to come, not only are the plagues going to run rampant there (they shall be in the water system), but when the drought comes forth, there will be murderers on the street who will rob your cupboards and slay you for only a sliver of bread. They are *dangerous* places indeed. If you cannot move to the western sphere, it is imperative, I urge you, to move out of your cities and seek you a place that has land. If the land is only large enough to support an elaborate lawn and flowers, dig it up and plant *food*. Wherever you live, I advise you to be *prudent*. Find your water source and *test* it. Do not take *anything* for granted. Become sovereign. Know your own progress. *Know* what you are doing.

Where are the grandest of places to live? The northwestern sphere. I have sent many people there, for even in the drought, there shall come the rains. And there, because of the temperature of the currents that flow into that area, the rains will be *pure*. No poison has fallen to rot away the forever green. The fishes still climb wildly up the streams. The bushes and brambles still produce their delicious, succulent berries. And the woods are wild and free, with game, food source. There, you can drink the water out of the ground, put your hair into a stream and wash it. It is the purest water there is.

Now, it is all right to live in the Midwest. But live where you have an abundance of trees. Live where you have water that is not tainted, that you can prick from the ground. Live where your land is utmost fertile for producing foodstuffs.

In the days to come within the Northwest, the storms prior to the lacking of rain will create great havoc. There is a depression already underway in the Midwest, not only in food, but also in resources. There, become *utterly* sovereign.

For those who are living in the Midwest, you will have increasingly ample sunlight. I advise and urge you to acquire solar converters and batteries. Do it! It will generate power. It will allow you to sustain. And if you are needing to pump your water, it will run your pump. If you cannot do that, affix a windmill—I will blow in gladdened gales!

Foodstuffs. Your stores have a great amount of food that is in metal and the like. That is very wise and very prudent. Buy up as much of that as you can. Plant gardens. If you do not know how to do it, *find someone* to teach you. These tools of survival will carry you through when others are falling like flies upon the land. Of that, *make haste*. Learn to produce and preserve your meats. Learn to collect your water. Learn to milk your own cow. You're going to need to. Indeed? *(Audience nods.)* And your clothing? Keep them.

Plant gardens. If you do not know how to do it, find someone to teach you.

Now, to those entities that are living in California: Which side of the zipper are you on? If you are on the beach side, you are going to find yourself in a pickle. If you are on the side of the zipper that extends itself east, you are in a very wonderful place. Those who live between the zipper and the coastline will be in direful straits in the days to come. And though you have planted wonderful lawns, you are advised, urged, and loved into planting some food and learning how to take care of yourself—for the sake of yourself, for the sake of your family. If you think you cannot leave where you are and have found many reasons why you should *not* leave, understand that you are in a gambling position.

In California, on the beach side, particularly now, you are urged to find your water source and test it. There has been a crack in your nuclear reactors that are close to there, and they are poisoning the ground. *This* you do not know. If you can leave where you are, *do* so. If it means going to the other side of the zipper, do so. There is a *vast* ocean of water that underlies the border of your state and the border of Arizona. Know you that state? The water that comes out of the ground there is immaculately pure. And there, you can irrigate and harvest, and find a new life. It is up to you.

If you are living on the beach line, understand what is coming. Know it! If you're resolved to stay, *make your peace*. For any hour that the pressure builds up greater on that zipper, you are going to have a *wonderful* quake. And it will blow off enough pressure to have adjusted a whole continent around.

Now, there is a great mountain in the north. She was named after a goddess. She is called Helen. Know you of her? She was beautifully symmetrical. She was captivating to the eye. And there were those who were drawn to her magnificent enigma. The entity became purposeful, for when she destroyed herself, she fertilized the land and salvaged your country once again. She is continuing to destroy herself to relieve the pressure that is building up from Nature's changing.

It is a fool who looks at wisdom and laughs at it.

Love yourself and understand this: It is a fool who looks at wisdom and laughs at it. Become mobile and do something about it. What if you don't think you can move? Do what you can where you're at. Be kind to yourselves.

There are those who will think this is absurd because they don't want to hear it. That is all right; it is their choosing. They are going to do what they want to do. Understand that.

Entities who are living further north are in a grand place, to be certain. But I advise the lot of them not to build their hovels near the water. That is not prudent. They are advised to go inland, near fresh water, and find a space of fertile land. There, they can live forever, for even in the severest of winters, it is an idyllic place. It is the remnants of my homeland.

With wisdom and knowingness, you will *know* what to do. And if Nature, in all of her splendor, decides not to expand her glowing self and create sunspots, what you will have done is still *wonderful*. You will have come full-circle: from sovereign gods who made their advent onto this plane, to limited man, to man waking up to *total sovereignty*.

Is it an accursed thing to have your larder filled? Is it an accursed thing to sit down to a meager meal and know you grew it, to know your energy produced it, to know you gave it life? Because it is thus, it will taste better and be much more nutritious than anything you have ever purchased from any market.

What is it that you find dreadful about being prepared? The ant is perpetual in its preparation *every year* that the seasons pass. Know you that in your great ice age, they survived? Know you that every animal life that had the qualities of hibernation and preparation survived to carry on, even this day in your time? It is purposeful sovereignty that I am speaking to you of, for I assure you, you are hard-pressed when you become a beggar, and you have given up your sovereignty to plea for help, for monies, for bread. One should never live like that. One should live in complete freedom, not austerity.

What is it that you find dreadful about being prepared?

(Walks over to the flowers and admires them) I *love* flowers. I have found them beautiful. I have watched them evolve. I have watched you create new species. It *gladdens*

me to see that. Never have I seen a rose like this in my lifetime. The roses of my time were sparse and few, and their petals, though fragrant and wild, were not as ''multudious'' as these that you have created.

There are many things to say on your behalf. Though you have done many things that have locked you into a limited life, you have done grand things also. You are wonderful creators.

Now, in reviewing what I have told you: All you have to do is to *want* to recreate your life. That is all. Just like you created this sublime, fragrant entity from a wild rose, you can do the same with your life *now*. All of you have the capacity to think and to feel. All you have to do is *want to*.

Now, I have heard your discussions and your feelings about my, what was it?, ''undying support'' for your King Reagan. *(Audience laughs.)* Aren't you happy that I can see in entities all of their grandness? I have seen all of his grandness, just as I see the grandness of you who complain about him. This entity is steadfast and was *destined* to be where he is. And for those in your country who cry out that they do not have enough money for social services, why do you want social services? If you want to be *free*, why are you depending upon your government to take care of you? Why are you squawking, and why are you hungry, and why are you uneducated, and why don't you *labor*? Because you have gotten weak in your spine and in your spirit, and you have become lax from letting everyone take care of you. And if they don't do it properly, you hate them.

If you want to be free, why are you depending upon your government to take care of you?

The grandest thing that this country will become is not a welfare state, but a country of integrity and human industrialism. It will become a nation where each takes care of his own, and the collective educates and supports their brothers without putting the burdens on politicians to please all of you! That is madness!

In the days to come, there will be *liberty*, and *all* will learn to find their genius and inspiration once again. That is desperately needed here.

If you give seeds to an entity who is hungry, and you do not teach him how to plant them, he'll eat the seeds. A new understanding is coming forward, and it is needed, for there are poor wretched entities in your beloved country who go to bed hungry every night. I am sending to them a wonderful light, and it will penetrate their dreams, it will penetrate their bellies. They, of themselves, are going to become an industrial *power*. I am going to see to it. So be it. *(Audience applauds.)*

Man's ability to change his attitude is the only thing that he has control over at this point. But then, that is everything. Through your attitude, you have contributed to the way your government is this day; you have contributed to the dissension in your streets; you have contributed to an unforgiving world with leaders bent on self-destruction. All of you have! Own up to it. For whatever think you, judge you, and fear you, you draw to yourself. Whatever judge you, you *are*, and you add that to the social structure of thought. You create the aura of suspicion and then draw those who are suspicious to you.

Everything you think in a limited, austere understanding affects all entities around the world. It is not *someone else's* fault that the world is in the state it's in. You have created your terrorists. You have created your mad rulers. You have raised monarchs, only to destroy them. You have voted in your presidents, only to hate them. You have created riots in your streets. You have the created bitterness of those abroad because you have added to all of it by how you think. Your world condition isn't just there! The collective attitude creates it and supports it.

It is not someone else's fault that the world is in the state it's in. You have created your terrorists. You have created your mad rulers.

Look! Even in this very divine audience, I watch you judge your food and the people who serve it to you. You are damning your food when you should appreciate it no matter *how* it comes! It is *food*, and it will sustain you. But you are complainers!

I have watched you judge others because of *their* attitudes. I have seen you blame others for your predicaments. What does that say about *you*? And what is that creating out in your world? It is creating *hatred*. It is creating the separation of brother from brother. It is creating insecurity in others, who become so fearful that they will seek to destroy you.

You judge others for the way they look or don't look. Well, not all people have flaxen manes and high cheekbones and clear blue eyes and figures that look like skin pulled over bones, but they are *all* beautiful. Whenever you judge someone for the difference in their appearance, you judge the *whole of the world*!

What I am saying to you is, your attitudes and your thoughts and how you are to yourself—and how that reflects to others in your own small world—has added to the misery of the whole. And I don't need to send a runner on this issue. You're going to draw to you enough of them to realize your own attitude, and they will reflect back to you how your attitude is affecting the world.

Masters, *everyone* is God—wherever they are, however they look, wherever they live—and they are loved as such. Whether they believe that understanding or not, *it doesn't matter*! They are *still* God and they are *still* loved.

There are people in your country who want to destroy the people of the Land of the Bear and the people of yellow skin because they don't believe in God. They are going to *destroy* them because they don't believe in God? It isn't important whether or how one believes in God! Whatever they believe, they are divine, because they live and breathe, they contemplate and doubt, and they are fearful *just like you*!

There are many grand entities who weep in your time. They are not national heros. They are not famous people. They are the sincere, the unknown, who have wept for the mercy of the world.

The hour of dissension is coming to a close. There is so much that Nature is going to be enacting, that man's mind is going to be taken off his distrust of his neighbor and his superior attitude toward others. He is going to be faced with survival, *base* survival, where you are hungry, and that's all you can think about. If it takes *that* to bring the world to a *common* pursuit, to a *common* link, *it will be worth it*.

Man is going to be faced with survival, base survival, where you are hungry, and that's all you can think about.

Who is worth judging? Who is not *worth* allowing. Hmm? What is your beef with them? Can't they do what they want to do? Can't you allow them the mercy and freedom to be their own selves? *Can't you*? If you are bent on changing a person, you must assess if you truly believe in your own ideals! Because when you are that way, it only means that you're not convinced of what you "know," and you're looking for support in numbers. Did you know that?

When you leave this audience and are heading back to your homeland, however you are traveling, look out at the world below you, around you, and above you. Look at it. Speak from the lord-god of your being and ask that the Father within all people come forward, and that the meek shall come into their rightful inheritance. Ask for peace to be mustered forward. Ask that the days of warlords and intimidators and despisers of the human element be *finished*, that they are *no more*. Then bless the whole of the world. When you have done that, you have done that for every cell in your body and every emotion within your soul and spirit, and the world will be *lifted* because of you. Get it? So be it.

Audience: So be it.

Ramtha: Now, the dissertation in regard to religion. Remember we spoke of this? I wish to clarify it. I do not despise religion. I don't despise *anything*. What I am saying to you is, be *aware*, not *ignorant*.

People all over your world are *steeped* in dogma, and it is a *malicious* experience. You only have to go to your libraries to discover this. You only have to look to your place called Ireland to know this. You only have to look at the Middle East to know this. You only have to look in your *own family* to know this. There are families who have turned their *own* members away because their religious beliefs were not the same as the family's. There are entities who speak in the name of God, and they have *damned* others *forever* because they did not do what the entities wanted them to do.

There is no physical place called hell that is burning in fire; there never was nor will there ever be. Even your dark holes in space, which some have suspected to be the eternal hell, are only passageways to a parallel dimension, a parallel universe, a different time flow. That is all they are.

There never was, nor ever will be, a Lucifer. He was created by the hearts and minds of man to poke, burn, intimidate and enslave *everyone* to a religious belief.

God is not good or evil. It is not perfect or imperfect. God is an *is*. In spite of dogma, God has *never* judged you, for it is the continuum called Life. Entities who speak in the name of God have always judged you, but God, the sublime, never has, for it has allowed and loved you, and *always* will. That continuum of divine understanding has *allowed* dogma, has allowed the wars, has allowed the rebukes, has allowed the condemnations. God is merciful because it is an allowing essence, and allowing equates *unconditional* love. God is unconditional because it is everything in its continuum called Forever. Let *no one* take that knowingness from you. No one!

Religion has inspired the murder of kings and queens; it has been "sanctioned by God." Whole armies have marched to their death under the auspices of a holy man, just to uplift his cause. Innocent children have had their eyes gouged out, just to get a confession from their mothers. The Jewish people have been despised all over the world for ages. They have been persecuted, burned, robbed, run out of their homeland, and they have never found a place of their own until recently. Were they not God? Of course they were!

This is *old* news. It has gone on for centuries. There was once a thriving civilization, which, though primitive, had its own wonderful spiritual understanding. This civilization is now extinct. Under the auspices of religion, its people were all murdered. They were labeled heathens, and their gold was robbed from them.

*What would bring one
so low
and make one
so callous
that he would murder you
because you will not
commit to his faith?
What sort of faith
is that?*

What would bring one so low and make one so callous that he would murder or destroy you because you will not commit to his faith? What sort of faith *is* that? If one does not have the same religious belief as you, are they not still loved by God?

This day in your time there are those who are being kicked

out of their religious organizations because they're not doing what they were told to do. At this hour, in the place called Ireland, a holy war has been raging for a century and a half *in the name of God*. In the name of God, entities are blown to bits. In the name of God, the streets run with blood. In the *Holy* Land, where all of the religions of the world have assembled their parthenons, their cathedrals, their synagogues, their huts, their hovels, they are suspicious and slanderous of each other. In a crib, a baby cries for its mother, who has been slaughtered because of her religious beliefs.

God allows all of this. One who is awakening, who, through common knowingness, *realizes* this, he realizes that God has never left *any one of them*, ever, ever, ever! He realizes that God has always been there; that you could not *possibly* be a bastard of the universe; that you truly *are* sons and daughters of the immutable, forever Cause.

The point I am making here is: Any commitment to any organization that despises, has disputes with, or does away with other entities because they are not "in the fold" should be looked at evenly. Evenly! If it isn't for you, *know* it. Regardless of whether someone condemns you according to *their* beliefs, you will still live forever. It is only when you accept their condemnation and *you* condemn *you* that you have lost it all. Regardless of how grand the rebuke that comes in your direction, love them, for that is being a light of the world; that is being God. Love them and allow them their truth. Only when enough loving has gone on, without *conditions*, will the world finally come out of the dream of its pagan beliefs.

Only when enough loving has gone on, without conditions, will the world finally come out of the dream of its pagan beliefs.

Now, there are, indeed, entities who are a part of religious organizations who are humble, who are fervent, who are *jewels*. They are, indeed, exalted of their faith. They have learned to be merciful. They have learned to love and to allow, regardless of religion or state, and they have worked for the grandness of mankind. They are sprinkled throughout every religion, but they are rare.

The hour of holy wars, of the persecution of your brothers for their beliefs, their faith, their God, is coming to an end.

And it *needs to*.

No one needs to preach to the world. That only leads to dissension, hurt, hatred, bitterness, and war. The world needs to be left alone. It needs to know that it is loved in a fellowship, and that is all. That is all!

I have been called many things. I have been called Lucifer. I have been called the Antichrist. I have been called everything that one can dig up that alludes to terrible, fearsome, horrible. That is their truth, and it has allowed me to see that their worship of "evil" is much grander than their acceptance of "good."

I love you, you wonderful entities who have ensnared yourselves for lifetimes, and who have found yourselves, in that snare, unequivocally unworthy. How could one *ever* feel worthy thinking that God has turned his back on you forever?

How could one ever feel worthy thinking that God has turned his back on you forever?

It's time to come full circle and become *aware* of the dream, the drama (oh! the drama). The fruitlessness of reliving life after life, again and again, should be wearisome to you. It is now the hour for *common reasoning*.

If you want to know anything, you don't have to look it up in ancient books. All knowledge is here and now, because it is *within you*. Whatever you want to know, just ask from the lord-god of your being and emotionally feel yourself *knowing* the answer. That is the power that will manifest the answer for you, and you will know. Then you are sovereign. Then you are free of this dream.

Understand the nature of people. Understand the nature of their convictions. Love them and allow them. If it means standing alone in your own truth and being true to the Father within you—if listening to *your* knowingness means that there shan't be anyone standing beside you, then *stand alone;* it will be *worth it!* Get it?

Love all who believe in whatever they believe in, and allow them their truth with grace. I beseech you, do not stand forward and war your truth upon them. If you do, you have become a dogmatic entity, an enslaver. Allow. *Allow*. When the light from you shines bright enough, they'll want to know what turned it on. Understand?

Audience: Yes.

Ramtha: I have not told you of all things that are going to come to pass. It is not that I hold out on you, but you have had enough of what has been given to you in bell-ringing clarity. Fortified with this wisdom, you can withstand everything. I assure you, the days to come will be ominous, indeed, to many people. Be jubilant, for it is *not* ominous; it is the grand adventure of a new world, a new consciousness, a new understanding, and peace. It is worth weathering anything to see Superconsciousness.

It is worth weathering anything to see Superconsciousness.

The understanding I have brought you, I have spoken evenly and clearly. If you did not hear it, it is by your choice. I respect your will and still love you in your decision.

Go wherever it *feels* right. Do whatever feels right, what rings in your soul. Be in a state of awareness and *trust* what you feel. Live *your* truth. It may not be the truth of your mother, your brother, your sister, your father, your lover, your husband, your wife, your children, but that does not mean that you're in error. Nor does it mean that *they* are in error. It simply means that you are honoring what you feel.

Solitude in sovereignty is absolute. You will never become sovereign in a group. You become sovereign *individually*. Unlimited, outrageous mind becomes only when one is wholly in tune with *self*. Get it?

Audience: Yes.

Ramtha: Now, what is the voice of God? Well, it is not your guides. Know you what they are? It is not your teachers, your crystal balls, your psychic fortune tellers, or your incense and rituals. Know you what those are? *(Audience does not respond.)* Well?

Audience: Yes!

Ramtha: All right! *(Audience laughs.)*

The voice of God does not speak in foreign tongues. It does not have a *high* voice or a *low* voice. It has *no* voice. The voice of God is *ultra-thought*, an extreme high frequency that triggers powerful buttons of emotions in your soul. You don't

You're getting caught up in metaphysics. That is only another dogma. Is that bewildering? It is a great truth.

hear it too often because you're so busy bombarding yourself with others' truths. You are busy running amuck, looking for whoever is going to tell you the best story of who you were in a past life. You're busy being caught up dogmas and rituals. You're getting caught up in metaphysics. That is only *another dogma*. Is that bewildering? It is a *great* truth. You are even getting yourself caught up in *this* teaching. You can quote what I say verbatim, but you have yet to *live* the *whole* of the teaching.

Masters, that ultrahigh frequency comes when you *allow* it to come. It has nothing to do with time or dimensions. It has everything to do with an emotion that sweeps you up. Ultrathought is a *feeling*. It is a wave of knowingness that you just know *instinctively*. There are no words to describe it, for words are limitations. They *utterly* do not define an emotion like this. It must be experienced. When you experience it, your are meeting God in his garden that is within you.

Many of you have not connected with this voice, for you have thought it to sound like everything else but what it is. Well, you are going to have to do a lot of *allowing* to hear that voice. You're going to have to create an environment that hums harmoniously. You are going to have to make the space for you to hear it. If you are blasting your music day in and day out, you're *never* going to hear it. If you can't work, labor, sit, or be in the *silence* of nature, you're going to have an arduous time hearing it. If you can't allow yourself to weep and be alone and be humbled, you'll never feel it. Get it?

That *sublime* emotion, I felt in my life—not until the later years of my life—only because I *allowed* it. And once I felt it, I *never* stopped listening. I had no teacher, no guide, no writings, no ceremony—nothing. It just came. So will it be with you who desire it.

I desire for you to know this and to reason it for yourself: *Whatever* you come up with, it is all right. Eventually you'll get down to the "nittus grittus."

Every moment, there are entities proclaiming new teachers, guides, spiritual truths. It's becoming rampant. And every moment, some entities are going to envision some catastrophe happening, and they are going to urgently want to get their truth out there. And that is why every moment there are entities leaving this plane into their next existence.

No one knows what you need to know. None of them! Not *one* of them can answer any of your questions earnestly. Everyone has an answer. Everyone in this room could close their eyes and open their mouths, and truth would issue forth. But how strong are you to manifest that truth and make it *happen*? How powerful are you? Can you "so be it" every runner into place? No.

There are those of you who are seeking out clairvoyants, oracles, guides. I desire for you to know that you are of a limited truth. For how can you say that God is supreme within you, that christ lives within you, when you have to ask someone else about your destiny, when you have to ask someone else for advice? Whenever you do that, you have only put yourself down and given your power away. If you want to seek out the advice of others, it is all right, but *that* is the next deadly religion. I tell you this because many of you still think that this is the thing to do. Well, go for it! But I assure you, you are never going to hear that voice. No matter *who* you go to or what they rant and rave about, it's not going to happen. You're never going to wake up and come out of this dream until you own up to your own immutable, illuminated divinity. If you scamper to someone to tell you what you *want* them to (and they will) in order to maintain your comfort zone, you're going to die. Know that.

You're never going to wake up and come out of this dream until you own up to your own immutable, illuminated divinity.

I tell you, *you* know it *all*. The days to come are going to *challenge* that very truth. You are going to have to know it, all on your own, because no one *else* will!

I love you. I desire for you to wake up and know how grand you are! I desire for you to embrace God, the Father within you, that intelligence, that *sublime* knowingness. To nurture the christ, the miracle worker, the king of kings, the power that no teacher could ever tell you about, you must simply *become it*. Then you are free.

It is not a horrible thing, masters, to say, "I know my own truth." It is deliciously arrogant—*and* it is *self-sustaining*. It is not a defacing of you to say, "I am becoming *all* that I can become, and I allow the Father within me to light my way." That is a divine thing to feel, to know, to embrace. But you'll never know that as long as you hang out your lives for someone else to take care of.

This truth this day will bring great joy and great release to many of your brothers in the days to come. And in spite of all small armies and their accusations at safe distances, this teaching will remain the grandest of all, and it will outlive all of its contemporaries, forever and ever.

This teaching will remain the grandest of all, and it will outlive all of its contemporaries, forever and ever.

(Raises his glass and toasts) To knowingness and the Father within, forever, and ever, and ever. So be it!

Audience: So be it!

Ramtha: Go and refresh, feed, water and relieve yourselves. And when the hour is at two, return unto this audience. Allow yourselves in this time *to be*. Find joy in everything.

I love you grandly, more than words in your common speech can express. You have learned greatly. I am exceedingly pleased, masters. So be it. That is all. *(The audience applauds warmly as Ramtha leaves the room.)*

***

Sunday Afternoon Session
May 18, 1986

Once the audience has settled in their seats, Ramtha rises from his chair and looks at them lovingly.

Ramtha: Where go I, my beloved brothren, when I leave this body and this august audience? It is called Forever. But from this sojourn with you, and from all that I am, beyond the enigma called "Ramtha The Enlightened One," I carry back with me, into Forever, a memory of you. For in the vastness of my soul, there is room for the whole of understanding *and* for you. I take you back into the bosom of God, where your face, your light, your thoughts, your memory, and these moments will be everlasting. And for that, I am exceedingly joyful. I love you!

I carry back with me, into Forever, a memory of you.

Audience: I love you.

Ramtha: (Raises his glass and begins the final toast. The audience repeats each line.)

From the lord-god of my being,
Come forth
Father within.
Open my mind,
Illuminate my path,
And bring forth wisdom.
Unto the christ,
O holy one,
Come forth,

That that which be I
And the Father within
Become magnified this moment
And for all times to come.
So be it!
(Toasts audience) To masters.

Now comes the moment of our sweet departure. Remember what I have taught you. Remember the runners when they come—and the ant. And for *all* that it is worth, *never* forget yourselves. Know that you are loved. Know that you are needed and appreciated. I will remember you for all times. So be it.

Go in peace. *I love you!* This audience and this Intensive are thus over. So be it! *(Audience applauds as Ramtha steps down from the platform and leaves the hall.)*

***

Appendix

Do You
Have Any Revisions?

Ramtha: Questions? *(Looks around audience at the raised hands)* Well, we have a few brave souls! Lady?

Woman: In May, you spoke of the days to come. I am interested in knowing if, perhaps, you have any, uh, *revisions* to your predictions. *(Audience laughs and applauds, and Ramtha laughs.)*

Ramtha: The deliverance of that message was to open up to you a window, so to speak, and have you take a look at what lies outside; and what lies outside the window is a shadow of the days to come. In other words, the sun is in back, and the shadow is seen first.

There are many runners that I sent you to show you that what I spoke is "right on." Do you remember them?

Woman: Yes.

Ramtha: Well, they will continue to come, on cue.

Now, what is wonderful in my being is that many did not see this teaching as something to *frighten* them into becoming sovereign. The teaching was seen as a grand opportunity and a realization to them that they were not sovereign. So, there are those who are now endeavoring, for the first time in eons, to become sovereign again. They are raising food to feed their bodies and realizing that what is most important is life. If one is endeavoring to *survive*, then one's priorities change very quickly, and one begins to see how fickle and fragile his illusions really are. When the ground begins to shake you out of bed, you are not going to think about ejaculations, or new auto

If one is endeavoring to survive, one begins to see how fickle and fragile his illusions really are.

machines, or personal crises; you are going to think about survival. Correct?

Woman: Correct.

Ramtha: Now, because of that teaching, there is a quickening in the consciousness here on your plane. Entities who have never even heard of me are suddenly desiring to put away foodstuffs. They are looking at their water. They are looking at their survival. They are desiring to change. Where is that desire coming from? It is coming from you who are enacting sovereignty. And that is *wonderful*, because it means that the whole consciousness is changing. You see? *(Woman nods.)*

Man, in his epic dream, has done many things to the earth for his own pleasure and convenience. Nature is now in a revolt; it is in the process of a forward thrust of evolution; it is healing itself. To one with a greater mind, this is seen as a great blessing and a great adventure. To those who are riddled with fear and who live as if there is no tomorrow, this is a terrible message. So, I am not prepared to speak evenly to all, because not everyone can comprehend this message—nor do they *want* to hear it. But what I have spoken is knowledge and a grand truth. Understand?

Woman: Yes.

Ramtha: Now, you desire to know about revisions, or changes, eh? In Nature, there will be two conditions coming together, almost simultaneously. Your earth's temperature is heating up due to the holes in your ozone layer, the destruction of your forests, and the pollutants and carbon dioxide that you have put in your stratum. What does this mean? It means the melting of the ice caps in the polar regions. That is already happening. Are you aware of this?

Your earth's temperature is heating up. What does this mean? It means the melting of the ice caps. That is already happening.

Woman: Yes.

Ramtha: Also, the pressure along the zippers will create pressure on the "vents," which are your volcanoes. Many of them are going to start waking up. When that occurs, your stratum will fill with dust and ash, which is very beneficial for the soil. But as long as the particles linger in the air, the light from the sun will not be able to get through. So, you will then have the *reverse* effect: you will then have a dramatic *fall* in temperature.

So, you will have two situations arising from Nature's changes that will create a polarity, and the flood waters from the melted ice caps will become ice again. An entity who can sense the changes and is moving according to knowingness will prepare himself.

The coming together of both of these situations is a reality. It is already happening. But from this, eventually, there will be a different climate here altogether, one that is very promising. Everything, lady, is on course. So be it.

Woman: Ramtha, I live in Michigan. I suppose that there will be flooding there.

Ramtha: Your Great Lakes that surround your state are fed, in part, by water from the great northern ice caps. Already there is a rising in the water level and devastation to the coastal lands there. The overabundance of water must go somewhere; so, in the days to come, there will be immense flooding of those areas. It is already underway. According to the actions of humanity, it will come very quickly or take a little while longer before it is completely flooded.

Tell me, lady, do you like where you live?

Woman: Yes, I am *very* happy there.

Ramtha: I desire for you to do this: With knowledge, you can prepare and plan accordingly. Put up your food and your water and your provisions as if you were going to take a long trip. If you are happy where you are, stay there, because if you are happy inside, entity, that will carry you through, whereas others might not survive.

If you are happy where you are, stay there.

If you don't want to move, if you want to stay where you are because you are happy there, then stay. But do take care of yourself and prepare as if there was a long winter coming. Understand?

Woman: Yes. I love you greatly, Ramtha. You've been my most *amazing* teacher.

Ramtha: Indeed?

Woman: Indeed. And it's good to see you in the physical

again. Thank you.

Ramtha: Just know and be wise, and follow your knowingness. It will *naturally* allow you to be prepared. Understand?

Woman: Yes.

Ramtha: So be it.

***

Tell Me When, Tell Me Where

Ramtha: (To a man in July, 1986) Master, indeed!

Man: I'm a commodities broker, and my wife and I moved from Iowa to California only two months ago. After listening to tapes of the Denver Intensive on Changes, we desire to move back to Iowa, what *now* feels like a safe place, as soon as we can. Even though I really didn't want to come to California, I did so because I didn't see any other way for me to survive financially in Iowa. But once I decided to come here, I did so with every ounce of enthusiasm and desire that I could muster. And I will leave here the same way.

Ramtha: Master, you say you are a commodities broker? What does that mean to you?

Man: It means that everything I do has a risk-reward ratio, and I speculate with—

Ramtha: Risk-reward? Is that gambling?

Man: Well, no. I'm willing to take *high* risks for *high* rewards. Gambling is a little different than speculation, but it's in that same—

Ramtha: Tell me, what are your commodities?

Man: Well, they are your grains, your meats, the buying and selling of "futures"—speculating on the future price of these commodities. So, I'm in the business of speculating the future.

Ramtha: Well, you are in a *very* wonderful business!

Man: Yes, I see that. But I have many things to do in order to be able to leave California, since I exhausted my savings in getting here. It's possible that in a few months, I could be in a financial position to leave, but I'm concerned about the timing of events. Is what you're predicting a matter of weeks or months? Will there be some more signs that you could show me so that I could "make hay" while the sun is still shining, but not be caught all of a sudden with nighttime while I'm still making hay? *(Looks around at the laughing audience for support)* Doesn't anybody *else* here want to know *when* this is going to happen?

Audience: Yes!

Ramtha: Master, time is an illusion. Do you understand that? *(Man nods.)* To predict an exact time frame is the greatest speculation there is, because many things must come together to bring about a specific change. So, to give you an exact hour cannot be done. But I can tell you precisely where the earth is *at this moment*—the proximity of the growth of the sun spots, the intensity of carbon dioxide in your stratosphere, the warming of your planet, the eruption of volcanoes, and the pressure on the zippers.

You are on the threshold of a major depression. If you say you do not know that, you are living in sublime ignorance, which most are.

Now, in regard to "making hay." By the fall of 1987, the situation will become very crucial. Already, master, your economic community is very aware that you are on the threshold of a major depression. If you say you do not know that, you are living in sublime ignorance, which most are. That depression has to do with the economies of the whole world, not only of your country. If you see a continuous depression of economic values by the fall of 1987, you are going to have *immense* problems, resulting in the possible collapse of your economic system. And this economic turmoil will be coupled with changes in Nature.

Man: Many of the research analysts who study economic cycles are saying something like that is about to happen, but I didn't see it happening in the next two or three months.

Ramtha: That is correct, but it has already begun. Its ramifications, as it were, flow into the *following* year.

Now, let me ask you: Do you *feel* that what I have spoken about Nature is a truth?

Man: Yes, I've felt it for a long time.

Ramtha: In being an entity who has made his pilgrimage to this country called California, do you realize that the earth has the ability to move under your feet?

Man: Yes.

Ramtha: If you stay here, you are going to continue to feel the rumblings of the earth. And a big, foreboding quake is but a moment away. That could happen at any moment. It is already set; it needs only the smallest catalyst. A major quake near the Azores is a sign that the one you are going to experience here is only moments away. A quake there will increase the pressure and the movement from west of your Pacific to your coastline. Your fault lines cannot withstand any more pressure. This country has already experienced rumblings; these should have been a sign to your scientists that a major quake is going to happen. But the exact time cannot be determined. That is Nature's explosive moment.

If you strategize your place *here*, make sure you're in a very solid place, in a solid structure on solid ground, far removed from the ocean. Then, perhaps, you can decide where you want to go after you reap the benefits of your commodities. Wheat "futures" is perhaps the greatest investment there is—other than the acquisition of what is necessary for surival: one's own land, water, and food.

How much time? You are taking a risk. If you are in tune with economics, then you must realize what is happening to your breadbasket, to your New England states, and to this state in particular. There are many events that will happen before the fall of 1987. They are all runners from Nature telling you, "Listen!" Many things have been telling you for a while that these things are coming, but no one has wanted to listen.

They are all runners from Nature telling you, "Listen!" But no one has wanted to listen.

Man: Thank you very much. That gives me a chance to prepare. I have another question. You've talked much about the safety of the Northwest region. Would you be more specific about where else in the United States it will be safe, or unsafe, to be? Also, what about countries south of the equator, like Australia and Brazil?

Ramtha: Your New England is suffering and will continue to suffer from poisonous ground water.

In the states of the Southeast region, where citrus is grown, their crops are in dire peril, and their climate is getting ready to change there. Also, it is not suitable to live there, since it is having a sinking problem.

In the Southern states, though there is some small relief because of the rain, the drought and the affliction of the economy there will be very desperate. Also, be wary of the ground water there.

This place, your California, is a beautiful country, but it is a very tenuous place because it draws its water from a foreign state. It is part of Nature's zipper, and it is moving. That is why I advise entities not to make a trek here.

Great places to be are the Midwest, the Canadas, Alaska, the Northwest, the countries called Montana, Idaho, Colorado, and the "new and improved" Mexico.

Great places to be are the Midwest, the Canadas, Alaska, the Northwest, the countries called Montana, Idaho, Colorado, and the "new and improved" Mexico. All of these places are good places to be, *provided* you are not near the coastline, you have your own well of pure water, you have put up your staples, and you are not near your great cities.

Now, underneath your world, in its southern regions: In Australia, because of its close proximity to the polar caps, you are going to see the land receding by the breadth of the water issuing forward. So, you will see a little *less* of that place.

In Brazil and South America, you are going to see weather patterns change from what was the rainy season to an unusually dry season. What is created in the stratosphere by you and your brothers will create the lessening of water, which will cause more rainforests to die in rapid succession. It will be like an oven there. There will also be earthquakes in those areas and the waking up of ancient, sleeping dragons called volcanoes.

Know you the reason that parts of South America are going to come under siege by Nature? The economy there is based upon the destruction of other entities. They grow plants [marijuana, cocaine] that were intended by Nature to be an easement of pain for animal life. They grow these plants abundantly there, and they are killing the people of this plane with them, for gold. Had these sources been obliterated, more entities upon this plane would have had a chance for joy. This assault upon your people has been a secret war of sorts to destroy your minds—and your *future* minds. It has had a *great* effect here! But what goes around is coming back. Very shortly there is coming a great plague upon that land and upon the peoples who are misusing this plant. Understand?

This assault upon your people has been a secret war of sorts to destroy your minds.

Man: Yes.

Ramtha: Those who are non-participants in that, who are the meek, who are are endeavoring to find peace in their souls and some sort of harmony with God, they will survive. So be it. That is all.

***

Should I Break Up My Family To Move?

Ramtha: Beloved woman.

Woman: I have two small children, and I'm ready to make a move. But my husband is absolutely *not* willing to go, and is not willing to listen to *any* of this. I've been upset and in a lot of confusion since May, and I'm asking you for some help—and the courage—to do what I need to do.

So, I want to ask you, do I need to break up my family in order for my children and me to survive to see Superconsciousness?

Ramtha: Tell me, where is your hovel?

Woman: I live in a place called San Rafael. It's about twelve miles north of San Francisco.

Ramtha: (Looks at her a long time) What would you *want* to do if you had any and all options? Would you stay with your husband even though *no* change was coming?

Woman: (Not so sure) I would *like* to. Um—

Ramtha: If nothing was impending, would you stay and be happy there? *Are* you happy?

Woman: It sort of fluctuates. Our relationship fluctuates. I've been trying to allow myself the freedom to do the things that make me happy, and also allow him to do the things that make him happy.

Ramtha: Is it working?

Woman: Is it working?

Ramtha: Indeed.

Woman: (Sighs and shrugs) Sometimes. *(Nearing tears)*

I'm also torn about taking my children away from their father.

Ramtha: What if you had no children?

Woman: (Resolutely) I'd be gone!

Ramtha: Why?

Woman: I want to be in a safer place. I want to be farther away from the cities, because that's the way I want to live.

Ramtha: You don't want to live in the city, then.

Woman: No.

Ramtha: If you had no children, would you still love your husband?

Woman: (Considers her answer) Yes, but I don't know if I would want to be married to him.

Ramtha: (Ponders for a moment before responding) Lady, you do not yet have the inner strength to make the change, because you would feel guilt over taking your children away from the opportunity to live with their father. And you would always blame yourself for everything that your children did that was without direction or discipline. "Safe" places do nothing for a soul that is troubled. No move, no change, does anything if you carry with you the burden of guilt.

"Safe" places do nothing for a soul that is troubled. No move, no change, does anything if you carry with you the burden of guilt.

(Sighs and looks at her compassionately) Let me do this: I will send some runners to your husband, and the runners shall be "newsworthy" entities. They will be scientists, and also his friends. Their talk of Nature's changes will be *greatly* exaggerated. This will begin to stir an acknowledgment in your husband.

Allow that opportunity to come. If your husband decides to become mobile, then your whole family may go and be happy and find a place of reprieve together, because the desire to do something about it will be with him also. If he does not decide to move, take care of your family and be on level ground. Put up all that you can for your family. Doing that ignites the emotion called love, the most powerful of all emotions—and *it* is the survivor of all things. And with a rapture of love for your tenure with your children and your husband, perhaps, in that light, safe ground can be found. In other words: Make the best of it. Do you understand?

Woman: Yes.

Ramtha: I love you, lady. Contemplate what I have told you this day.

Woman: I will.

Ramtha: So be it.

***

How Can I Sell My House To Some... Poor Sucker?

Man: (Following a discussion with Ramtha about moving from the fault line in the San Francisco area) I would like to sell my house. Is there any way this can be done in the next few months?

Ramtha: Master, how do you feel about selling your house —when you know the things that are coming?

Man: (Sheepishly) Well, I was planning to sell it, *anyway*. I've been wanting to get out of the salmon fishing business for a year now. What you've said about the coming changes is just giving me a kick in the rear. I've definitely decided that I want to move up north.

Ramtha: Do you have any difficulty selling your house to some "poor sucker"?

Man: (Shaking his head) That's a very hard thing to answer. It *is* a beautiful place to live. But I don't know. That's a hard thing to handle.

Ramtha: Well, maybe I can help you "handle it." I desire for you to do this: Be impeccable. Do things *impeccably*. This "sliding stuff under the rug" stinks! And it will haunt you.

Be impeccable. Do things impeccably. This "sliding stuff under the rug" stinks! And it will haunt you.

If you desire to sell your house, I will send you a couple of runners. But I desire for you to tell them that the reason you are selling it is that you are moving up north because this problem with earthquakes has really gotten to you. Isn't that the truth?

Man: Well, I would say that that's *part* of the reason. I came from the Northwest to start with—from Seattle in 1932.

Be impeccable to the potential buyers. Tell them that you feel that where you live is not suitable for you because of the earthquakes and all.

So, the reason that we're relocating is not only from your teachings, but for other—

Ramtha: But, master, to be *impeccable* to the potential buyers, tell them that you feel that where you live is not suitable for you because of the earthquakes and all; that you would rather sell the place and leave. Your area is known for earthquakes, is it not? Is it a secret?

Man: No, everyone knows it.

Ramtha: If you tell the potential buyer why you desire to move, and they smile at you and nod, because they don't have a problem with that, let them sign on the dotted line.

Man: Well, that's what I will do then. I won't be pulling a "fast one" that way. Just like my boat's not a perfect boat. If somebody wants to buy it, they buy it "as is."

Ramtha: So be it.

***

There Is Land Everywhere

Man: I have just returned from a two day climbing trip on Mt. Rainier, and it was a grand adventure. The sunrise was beautiful above the clouds, and our guide said it was unusually *windy*.

Ramtha: Of course. *(Audience laughs.)*

Man: And we saw *spectacular* cloud formations on the top as we came down.

Ramtha: Isn't it all rather splendid?

Man: Indeed.

Ramtha: Master, one hasn't truly lived until he has seen the mountains and the valleys, has been caught up in the clouds, or has had icy snow blown in his face. Indeed?

One hasn't truly lived until he has seen the mountains and the valleys, has been caught up in the clouds, or has had icy snow blown in his face.

Man: Yes. It was beautiful, and—

Ramtha: It is, but there are so many who haven't even been outside their wretched walls! It's just too big an effort! And they wonder why they are so miserable.

Pardon the intrusion; do continue.

Man: You've often said that the Northwest is a good place to live, and I am thinking of moving there. But I understand that Mt. Rainier is a volcano. Is it going to go off or not? I notice that JZ and many others live near it.

Ramtha: Master, it is a divine mountain, and it will stand. The energy that is collecting itself there is in harmony with Nature. There, the trees are allowed to stand, and they keep the air clean. There, the fish are still allowed to perpetuate their future, you can go out and eat a berry off a bush, and you can still expect the rains to come (and blessed are those succulent drops from heaven!). Because of this environment, the mountain is in a beautiful nest. And it, looming in its rapture of white, will become a symbol—of freedom.

If Nature ever decided that the mountain needed to be sacrificed, for whatever reason, it will go, just like anything else.

Now, it *could* change. If the consciousness ever shifted, or if, in its natural evolution, it *needed* to change, it would do so. If Nature ever decided that the mountain needed to be sacrificed, for whatever reason, it will go, just like anything else. That is up to God, Nature, Life. But as it is seen this hour, for many eons to come, it will stand. So, you may do whatever you wish. If it feels right, move there; if it doesn't, go elsewhere. It is up to *your* knowingness. Understand?

Man: Yes, thank you.

Ramtha: Now, this is for all to know: I have been asked by my daughter to give you a message. She desires for me to engage you to know that the wee little township where she has formulated her life with her husbandman and their few *thousand* (!) head of horses *(audience laughs)*, they chose for their home a long time ago. Because they are there does not mean that it is sacred ground. And the little township wouldn't be a little township any longer if the lot of you barged in there.

There is land everywhere outside of that province. Use your *own* knowingness to find where *your* place is. Do not move there because they are there. Get it? Go where it feels *divine* —to *you*.

She desires for you to know that you are *greatly* loved, but she wishes for you to understand this. That is the end of the message. So be it.

***

You Have Made Your Own Answer

Woman: After I attended your Intensive on Change, I went back to my home in the Southwest and contemplated leaving that area. But when I talked to my husband, I found that we have different feelings about what to do in preparation for these times. So, I have two questions. I want to know how the water situation is in the Southwest. It is really dry down there, and I'm not so sure it will be a good place to live.

My other question centers around our economic system. Will there a different economic system in the times to come? Will we even *have* an economic system, or will we be living independently of one, trying just to survive?

Ramtha: Regarding your first question, didn't you answer that for yourself?

Woman: Well, not everyone agrees with me, but I know how *I* feel. It doesn't seem like a good place to me. It seems pretty dry there to me, especially after being here in Seattle this week.

Ramtha: What does your knowingness tell you?

What does your knowingness tell you?

Woman: I feel like I'd like to move farther north, but I don't know if that is *knowingness* or if it's just desire.

Ramtha: And your husbandman?

Woman: He wants to stay where he feels there is work for him. I am willing to take a chance that we will find a way, no matter where we are.

Ramtha: But your husbandman?

Woman: Well, I may have to leave him behind.

Ramtha: Lady, when you listened to my audience, did you respond in fear or the desire to survive?

Woman: (After pausing to think) I feel as though I responded out of the desire to survive. To me, it's really exciting to contemplate change, and I got very excited about the prospect of a new life. I decided that I would like a change even if nothing was going to happen in the world. I really would like to change everything and move from the part of the country where I am now living.

Ramtha: What if you compromised? What if you put up foodstuffs sufficient for two years, drilled a well for your own water, and created a holding tank to store it? Do you understand how that works?

Woman: Yes.

Ramtha: If you did that, and could weather the storm, as it were, would you stay?

Woman: I'm not sure.

Ramtha: Do you *want* to stay?

Woman: I don't think so.

Ramtha: Why?

Woman: I don't know. It just doesn't feel right.

Ramtha: So, if you had everything that you needed to survive there, it still wouldn't feel right?

Woman: No, it wouldn't.

Ramtha: Then you have answered your own question.

Woman: Yes, I see. Thank you.

The economic system will be drastically different, little resembling the economic world of business today.

Ramtha: Now, the answer to your other question: In Superconsciousness, the economic system will be drastically different, little resembling the economic world of business today. The importance of knowing survival, however, is going to be imperative past your year 2010. Many, many things will happen before that year; but after that time, entity, you will see a renaissance of a Light Age.

Surviving may sound like hard work to many of you, but there is a grand and ancient, primeval feeling in one who nutures the survival of his own being, who can manifest his own food and water, his own shelter, and his own clothing. There is a grand reward in coming back to that quality of life. And in survival, there is a purging in oneself and a simplicity that allows you to build the strength of character and of mind so that your mind will have the ability to open up to a new consciousness and a new age. And the economics of that age will have nothing to do with gold, but everything to do with *light*.

The present consciousness is lazy; that is why it has slipped into decadence; that is why it is at war with Nature. But your "kamikaze lifestyle" is coming to an end.

Your kamikaze lifestyle is coming to an end.

That answers your questions. But get set for a long haul.

Woman: I will. Thank you.

***

The Fallible Dream

Ramtha: (Addressing the audience at the Intensive on Financial Freedom held on March 14, 1987) So, you're all here after money! *(Audience laughs and applauds.)*

In my innocence, I have asked those who have come unto my audience, "What desire you, master?" And they would say to me, "Ramtha, I desire to be God." And *then* they would say, "And I also want to be rich!" *(Audience laughs.)* So, I am cutting through all of that, eh? You're all here to get money, what I term "gold."

"I desire to be God. And I also want to be rich!"

Now, gold has always had a value on your plane, for it is a tender, shiny, wondrous metal of great rarity and beauty. It is a soft, sensitive metal that absorbs emotional frequencies. Put on the gold breastplate of a king, and within moments you will feel his preeminence, his glory in wearing it, because his emotion is locked into the metal. In other words, gold is liken unto the soul, for it holds emotions. In that regard, it is the greatest of all metals; that is its value. Understand?

Audience: Yes.

Ramtha: Now, there are those of you in this audience who surmise that your every problem would be taken care of if you just had enough . . . *(waiting for audience to complete his sentence)* Well, speak up, hypocrites!

Audience: (Laughing) Money!

Ramtha: Indeed. Now, there are a few of you sitting with your arms folded, and you are thinking to yourself, "That's not me at *all*. How tacky of him to say that! All *I* want is a better paying job.'' Well, when you say that, you're only cleaning up the thought a little. In the core of your dreams, you still think that money, or gold, is the answer to all of your prayers. Everything revolves around it. So how do I teach you that it is far greater to replace the desire for gold with the desire for *genius*, the mind that can create it all?

If every one of your dreams is based on money, you are in for a very rude awakening.

Now, I am telling you this for a reason. If every one of your dreams is based on money, you are in for a very rude awakening. If you are counting on your investments or your stock market to fulfill your future and your dreams, you are on very tenuous footing because your world is in the throes of bankruptcy. Your nation has a greater deficit than you know.

Listen to me: Your paper money is not *your* money! It is owned by the Federal Reserve, which is owned by *international* bankers composed of the most powerful families since the hour of Napoleon. They have no allegiance to any country or to any people. Their allegiance is only to profits. There is a conspiracy of sorts to break the backbone of your middle class so that there is wealth for only a very few, who will govern all of the ''rabble,'' you.

Your money is not owned by your country. I was amazed to see how many of you think that because it says ''Federal,'' it means your government owns it. Well, it doesn't. The Federal Reserve is owned by these entities, who even create wars to gain power and control over human destiny.

Your country doesn't go to war because of a noble virtue. It goes to war because it's good business! Don't you understand that!?

Your country no longer has the gold to back up its paper money. And when gold no longer backs up your money, you are treading on thin ice, because then these entities can dictate how much, or how little, your dollars are worth. Then you are . . . *(holds out his empty hands)*

Audience Member: Wiped out!

Ramtha: Wiped out? Hungry! Wanting. Needing. Hurting. Unhappy.

Know you that it is not you who create inflation/deflation.

It is not you who create rises and falls of your stocks and bonds. It's all an illusion. International powers, the ones who own the money, sit around your wondrous globe like players in a chess game, and they pull the strings.

International powers, sit around your globe like players in a chess game, and they pull the strings. But their hour is coming to an end.

Why does this situation exist? Because these entities are gods, just like you are, and they are playing out *their* dream. Do you understand? It is what they are needing for *their* learning. But their hour is coming to an end.

So, it seems that you are in a pickle. What should you do? Now that you are *aware* of the situation, begin to assess what it is you really want, and whether you desire a dream that is not so fallible. In other words, isn't it far greater to be able to manifest what money can buy rather than the money to buy it? When you learn to embrace the desire of what you want the money to purchase, you'll get it, lickety split—*without* money. Understand?

When your vision is always focused on your desire to have more money, you close down your awareness of your other possibilities. If all you want is money, you are going to die an unhappy entity, I assure you, and it will mean *no thing* the moment your spirit calls your soul from the body.

So, here we have you who are blatantly ignorant about how your economic system works, who are very naive about power. And here we have you who have spit in my eye when I said, "Put away food," because you want what "really" counts. Money!

Well, one day, grasshopper, you'll be sitting outside the ant's door, knocking.

***

Golden Opportunities

Woman: Ramtha, I've been keeping a very close eye on what's going on with our economic system. I'm really clear that the financial breakdown is very close, as you have said. Yet I feel a need, or a compulsion, to do many things that I have been dreaming about, and I'm concerned that I will not have everything done by the time the changes occur. I keep thinking a lot about this, and it's creating a lot of mind churning in me.

Ramtha: Indeed, woman. I realize that it's rather disappointing for entities who had all sorts of hopes and dreams about their careers and their futures to learn that many things may not exist as opportunities.

Now, your government *is* going into financial collapse. It is already there; it is just a matter of the final agony. But there is *purposefulness* in that, because a balance needs to occur, a reorganization as to value. In that, opportunities are going to change, dramatically.

I know what your dreams are, lady. They are many. Well, you *will* realize your dreams, but perhaps not in the limited *fashion* that you imagined them. You will realize your dreams in an *un*limited way, more grandiose and more vital than you ever imagined.

You will realize your dreams, but perhaps not in the limited fashion that you imagined them.

To many, this sounds like the end of the world. To others, it is just a beginning. Of course, it's a matter of one's perception. But the opportunities will be *vast*, I assure you. You understand?

Woman: Yes. Thank you. Also, can you tell me when the monetary system might collapse? In the future, will there be any kind of money that's of any value?

Ramtha: As it is now seen, your stock market will collapse around May of 1988. Your dollars and coins that are not silver will become worthless. In the collapse, your dollars will have value as low as seven cents. Your gold will—how do you say? —"reach the heavens."

In the republic that is coming, there will be no need for money. But in the cross-over time, gold—actual gold, not *paper* gold—will increase in value. By the latter part of September and into October of 1987, you should already have bought some gold, even if it is only five one ounce coins. That doesn't mean that you cannot purchase coins through the end of your year, but as it is now seen, your greatest opportunities come in those months. Increasingly, gold will be very difficult to come by, because your government will confiscate the majority of it to back its existence. Do you understand?

Gold will be very difficult to come by, because your government will confiscate the majority of it to back its existence.

Woman: Yes.

Ramtha: So, in the latter part of your country's financial collapse, you can take your gold and free yourself of your mortgage and your obligations. Then you will have no indebtedness, and the carpetbaggers will not come to take away all of your possessions. You will be free. Understand?

Woman: Yes. Thank you.

***

They Are Your Brothers, Not Your Saviors

Man: Ramtha, recently there seems to be an increase in the number of UFO sightings and abductions by aliens. Also, there seems to be an increase in the number of people channeling extraterrestial beings. I was wondering if there is anything you might like . . . *(Ramtha throws back his head and roars with laughter)* . . . to, um, share with us concerning this.

Ramtha: A new dogma, eh?

Man: Ramtha, I *understand* the idea of not turning these things into a religion. I *do* understand that, but I just felt I should ask this question, for the group. *(Ramtha bursts out laughing again.)* There *are* a lot of people interested in this. You know what I mean?

Ramtha: Indeed, master.

Man: Are these extraterrestials just *watching* us, or are they planning to help us through the days to come?

Ramtha: Help you? Why do you think you need help?

Man: To get beyond social consciousness, I guess.

Ramtha: Master, know you the term "spinning your wheels"?

Man: Yes.

Ramtha: As if things weren't troublesome enough, now you are concerned about aliens sitting up in spaceships somewhere; and you're wondering whether they are going to intervene and save your skin. And if they *are* coming, you are *hoping* that you will be in the right place at the right time to be picked up. Correct?

Man: Well . . .

Ramtha: Master, let me give you a truth. If you don't like it, if you don't want to own this truth, or if you insist on having a different one, then, by all means, go for it!

The entities in these ships are your higher brothers. Now, by "higher," I do not mean that they are *greater* than you; they are just high up in the sky somewhere, that is all. Nothing different, same game. These "aliens," as they are termed, do exist, and they do come here. They come from other stars, other dimensions, and even from the center of your earth. They drop in and out here, just like your country visits the moon. They are beauteous entities, indeed. Many, many of them in their cultures have gone far beyond war, pestilence, and disease because they are open-minded entities. Many of them have looks that differ greatly from yours, that you would term ugly to look at because you judge beauty to be the outward dimension.

These entities are your *brothers*, not your saviors, yet they are being worshiped on a massive scale here because of the many myths that surround them. To think that one of them is speaking *through* you is most glorious, mysterious and awesome, but it is also hogwash! If they *want* to talk to you, they can do so directly. They don't need an intermediary channel to do it. And if they wanted to show you that they really are real, they could plop right down in your own yard and have dinner with you. You know, if you *really* want to make contact with an intelligent mind, try channeling an ant! They have a better understanding of what is going to happen, how to get things organized, and where to dig in, than any other creature. Understand?

If you really want to make contact with an intelligent mind, try channeling an ant! They have a better understanding of what is going to happen, how to get things organized, and where to dig in, than any other creature.

Man: Yes.

Ramtha: Mankind is getting ready for an immense "battle," called survival. There are a lot of people who want to stir up the pot by making news and saying that these entities will intervene to save you, that they're going to pick up the "chosen few." Well, what about that poor sucker out in the field who is waiting to be picked up when all hell is breaking loose? What are you going to tell him when it doesn't happen?

Master, unless something can put bread on your table, unless it can challenge your mind into living *here-and-now*, into living in *joy*, or into understanding one's *sovereignty*, it's of no importance. It is just another idol, another game, another illusion. There are *many* things that I *could* teach you, and many wonderful adventures you could go on, but mankind is not ready for them, for he hasn't unglued himself from the bonds of idol worship, and he hasn't released himself from the glamor and excitement of fear. He gets off the track by always looking to things "out there" instead of taking a hard look at what's inside.

When you get beyond the need to look outside yourself, you will find peace and alignment with all things. Then you will know of all wonderful things. And you won't know of them *second hand*, because then you will be in the flow of all life. Knowledge, reasoning, knowing that God is within you and touching the hem of that divinity—that is your only salvation. Do you understand?

Man: Yes.

Ramtha: There are so many things that you utterly take for granted. If you spin your wheels in search of bright lights in the sky, you are never going to appreciate the beauty of the earth you are standing upon or the beauty of the one who is looking for them. It is a wise and prudent entity who undertakes the discovery of *self* and his *own* environment before he casts his eyes to the "beyond" into forever. Only when man accepts and owns all of *his* life and all of his yesterdays, is he ready to go forward into Forever, because then there is no longer the pain of regret or the desire to look back. You have fully experienced and embraced the whole of this life here, and you have the wisdom of it locked in your soul.

It is a wise and prudent entity who undertakes the discovery of self and his own environment before he casts his eyes to the "beyond" into forever.

There have been many landings of these entities, and there will continue to be. If contemplating them gives you a thrill, that is all right. If, by chance, one lands in your back yard and desires to parlay with you, parlay if you wish; but don't fall on your face and prostrate yourself in front of them. And don't live for the day that contact might occur, lest it never happens. Because if it doesn't, what can you say that your life has been for, eh?

You know, entities say that I get real "down" on things. No. I just make sense of them.

These entities are not planning to land and take you away. And be glad for that, because what is *their* paradise may be a fright to you. And besides, there are only a few places in the whole of the universe that your biological being, as it is now, could even survive. Before they could take you away on their ships, they would have to pack you in a jelly-like substance just to keep you from falling apart, and most ships are not large enough to facilitate those sorts of needs.

In regard to abductions: These entities know about spirit, God, and foreverness. They possess the knowledge of light and the technology that allows them to be inter-dimensional and inter-stellar. If they possess the knowledge of these things, what do they need *you* for? In other words, with all the problems, woes, limited thinking and bigotry in your life, why would they want you to pollute theirs?

With all the problems, woes, limited thinking and bigotry in your life, why would they want you to pollute theirs?

Now, since they know about all of these things, why *have* they abducted and examined some of you? Because they haven't *been* you. Mankind is a mystery to them because they have never lived as one of your species. They desire to understand how your biological and physiological systems work, so they search for answers. You must admit that you are a peculiar group. It is a puzzlement to any *great* mind to understand why *yours* isn't working! Now you know why they don't sit in their starships and try to channel one of *you*. This is not a put-down, only the truth.

So, you are a mystery to them. Many of them come in and out of your stratosphere from bases on the dark side of the moon. They have made contact with many entities and they have examined some of you to learn about you. And if they wanted to destroy you and your world, they could have done so long ago; they're that powerful. But they are also that loving, for they exist in Superconsciousness. They are experiencing the next forever adventure.

These entities have been here before in large numbers, and they have taught your ancient civilizations. Do you know why they have not come to teach *this* great civilization? Because this "great" one just isn't so great. I shudder to think what limited man would do with the understanding of more advanced technology. With *your* pettiness of mind and *their* technology, your solar system would quickly become only a large rim of dust, for you would certainly destroy yourselves.

Why have entities from other stars systems returned to your plane throughout your history? Because they are on a great sojourn, a grand adventure. Forever is a big place, and they stop back here every now and then to say hello and to see what you've been doing for, say, the last 10,000 years or so. It's sort of like going back to the zoo and seeing the new selection of species. Get it?

Man: Yes. Ramtha, do you think it will be possible to visit the inner earth after we've learned to survive and have come out of social consciousness?

Ramtha: Master, what you are going to live through is not going to *reward* you with visits to alien civilizations. What will become of the human race from the times that are coming will be the beginning of a race of entities who will be more liken unto your brothers in these ships that you contemplate. Mankind will be a race of entities who are without bigotry, prejudice, and limitation. It will be a brotherhood of the meek, and they shall, indeed, inherit this plane, for only those of such consciousness will choose to live here.

Until then, begin the adventure of knowing the most alien entity of all, *you*, because that is what you must do if you desire to be a part of the days to come. Understand?

Begin the adventure of knowing the most alien entity of all—you!

Man: Yes. Thank you.

Ramtha: If you do that, I assure you, master, you are going to see some most *remarkable* things in your lifetime. Your UFOs shall only be a very small and inconsequential part of them. So be it.

***

The Black Plague

Ramtha: This pertains to your tomorrow.

There was a year in your counting; it was called 1348. And there was a place called Europe. Know you where that is? It is sort of a conglomerate of diffused boundaries. Well, there was a great war within many of these boundaries, and the war was the war of Catholicism against Judaism. That which was Catholic did not like that which was Jew, for they blamed them for *crucifying* their Lord. And yet Yeshua ben Joseph had said, "Behold! I have come to *fulfill* the prophesy." Without what happened at Jerusalem, Yeshua *never* could have achieved that. They forgot that.

During these times, the Jews within these countries were being forced to convert to a religious belief, Christianity. Those who did not convert were hated by the people who were the "good" Christians, who then slaughtered, mutilated, maimed, burned, and destroyed them. (Very "godlike," wouldn't you say?) All through this place called Europe, the air was polluted with the stench of burning carcasses and bloody, mutilated, rotting bodies on the road. (Perhaps that is where the devil was "born" and where "hell" got its deepest meaning.) Whole groups of frenzied, fickle people rioted and participated in the murder of Jews because someone told them that if they did that, God would *love* them.

All throughout Europe, the air was polluted with the stench of burning carcasses and bloody, mutilated, rotting bodies.

A most peculiar thing happened in 1348. There came on the shores of that continent a horrid thing. A disease was born. It came out of *nowhere*, and it consumed over 25 million people, one-third of the population, in just one decade. This most odious of plagues did not have religious preferences. The Church said it was a curse of God upon the heathens, but the Christians died too. It ate away at the Catholics, it ate away at the Orientals, it ate away at the Jewish people. It had no religious preferences. The only preference it had was that it devoured only those with the attitude of hatred, bigotry and decadence.

Now, in your light, you are "known" by your attitude. And magnetically, you draw to you what you are. That is the *law*, because you are God. That is why the plague consumed only those entities.

The plague, called the Black Plague, was a reprisal from Nature against those whose attitude had collapsed below the survival level. You can war against Nature just so long before it declares war on you. In other words, Life is going to get rid of those who do not go forward. So, the disease got rid of them, one-third of the population.

You can war against Nature just so long before it declares war on you.

So deadly was this disease that they had to turn their attention away from their bigotry to base survival. They had to *redefine* what was important.

Now, you use barely one-third of your brain. Did you know that? And one-third mind is the lowest point man can fall to before the human race becomes extinct. In other words, you are now *below* survival. Your society is into decadence, perversion. You rape your children. You defile your women. You men molest one another. You brutalize sex, eroticize violence, and you sell fear in the marketplace—and you are *insensitive* to it! When you are insensitive to it, it means you are living in decadence, below survival.

In 1348, they too were below survival; they had slipped into decadence. What kind of an entity beheads a babe because its mother will not convert? Hmm? That is not being concerned with *survival*; that is decadence! Well, you have slipped into decadence liken unto that of the year 1348.

You are all God. And when gods begin to have inward collapse, so comes what I call the "War of Valued Life." There are plagues now upon your land; and from those plagues are growing more plagues. They will never be cured, and they will take from the world one-third of your population before the end of your next decade. That is how it is seen at this moment in time.

These plagues aren't something that comes from outer space! *You created them!* Your body is trying desperately to keep you together, but you are tearing it apart by always criticizing it! It is either too fat or too thin or too old or the wrong sex. When you do that, what is your body going to do with you? It can only stand so much pressure. Either it's good enough or it isn't! If you don't allow it to be what it is, it's going to get rid of you. A little plant with a frog upon its leaf, the caterpillar and the butterfly, the black stallion with fiery nostrils—it is the life force within them that is declaring war on you, because you are corrupting and impeding the evolutionary process called Forever. And in that war, masters, Life will win, always.

Your body is trying desperately to keep you together, but you are tearing it apart by always criticizing it!

The plagues are now here, and you created them, because you are degrading your body and spirit; you are collapsing inwardly. Thus you are going to die.

Ominous? In some ways it is, depending upon how limited you are. The plague is here, and there are many who will not escape it, because they will not get out of the boxes of social consciousness to become Life again. That is the *only* way that you overcome it—through virtue, noble virtue.

This is an important topic that has been evaded by many. You have been patronized, stroked, and complimented into dying. You have not had to face history, soul memories, and your ''now'' in such a vivid and painful understanding.

So, that is your destiny, as it is seen this moment. Now *what* did I just say? *As it is seen this moment*. Your destiny is seen because the shadow of it is cast by your attitudes. Everything you think manifests, and the plagues are the *result* of your thinking, your attitudes, if you will. In the tomorrow of your time, the whole of the world *could* be lifted by a grand experience—at least up to the point of survival.

When you come back up to survival, the disease will go away. You have the power to change it at any moment.

Your consciousness has fallen below survival into decadence. When you come back up to survival, the disease will go away. You have the power to change it at *any moment*.

How do you change this most ominous shadow? By *loving* what you are. Loving yourself means to hold yourself in the grandest and highest of esteem. It means to *know* you are endowed with divinity, to know you are endowed with a greater mind, to know you are brilliant and that you possess genius. Loving yourself means to know that you are, above all, endowed with life. Life! Without it, you are a no thing.

You women, for so long you have survived because of your uterus, your vagina, and your breasts. Your body has been your survival. Stop giving your bodies away. It is the hour that you say that you will survive because you are embracing *life*, as an equalness in God. That is loving what you are. When you learn to love yourself, you will not need to grab hold of someone else to make you happy or to take care of you. Then you are free, independent.

And men, you don't have to go out and copulate everything to impregnate the whole world! (In your soul memory, that equates being a man.) You don't have to spill your seed every single day! Every moment you do that, you are *dying*. You have to master the desire to molest children for a thrill. You must master the desire to molest your brothers so that you feel you have power over them. When you master those things, that is loving who you are. See women as equals, as brilliant gods, just as you are. That *changes* the shadow, the destiny; that allows you to go forward in harmony with Nature.

In 1348, when the plague had finished its ravages, a new consciousness appeared. It was a new understanding, a change, a difference. It is the same with this age that you are in. When the decadence that is now upon this plane has left, there will emerge a new consciousness and a new mind. It is called Superconsciousness. The mind will bloom, and the christus in *all people* will come forth—the realization in all people that they are God. That is the true meaning of the second coming of Christ: "And behold, there came forth a new kingdom and a new earth. And in that kingdom reigns the Christ, forever and ever and ever.''

This is the destiny of your good earth.

***

Looming On The Horizon

Ramtha: I have something I would like to ask you, and I desire for you to "bend your mind." Contemplate this and be sincere with you, eh?

So . . . the Days of Change are now *looming* on the horizon, and the adventure that lies therein is yet to be experienced. And you are looking toward that horizon.

You have busily worked to create for yourself a state of undeniable survival. You packed away "the goods." Know you "the goods"? The staples of life, and your water. You were hard-pressed to do it, but now you have quite a collection. How *wonderful* it is to know that come-what-may, you have provided for the enigma *looming* on an uncertain horizon.

(Looks at the audience) You're getting this? *(They nod.)*

You left your potentially vulnerable area because, through pure reason, you realized the desire and the necessity to do so. You made a swift deal on your high-rise condo in a most fashionable area. You sold your hovel on the ocean, the one you dreamed of having all of your life. (Lord knows what you did to get it!)

You transferred from your corporate home office to some backwoods facility that lacks all the class, the drama, the intrigue that you had before.

You cashed in your life insurance policy, kissed your family good-bye, and made your sweet partings.

You have been, oh! so persevering. With great diligence, you have put yourself on safe ground, and you are dug in for the run! Are you with me?

Audience: *(Laughing)* Yes.

Ramtha: Now, contemplate this: You are watching the horizon. You're watching it, and you're watching it, and it's just sort of . . . *sitting* there. Looming. Foreboding. And what was once an exciting sojourn of preparation has become . . . impatience!

"Where is that friggin' tidal wave?"

"Happen! I want to see the *earth* split *open*! Where is that *friggin'* tidal wave!?" *(Shrugging off the laughter)* Well, they're *your* words! And you continue to look toward the horizon, and lo and behold, you see . . . nothing. Nothing! *Nothing!*

You're getting letters from home. "Just returned from shopping. Had a wonderful lunch! Mom's okay, kids did great in school. Bought a new auto machine. Should see it! Wish you were here!"

All of a sudden the economy takes an upward swing. Employment is up. The stock market is wonderful! But there are rumors of war in the East. (Well, that's a *sure* sign that nothing has changed!) Your country is still trying to send rockets to forever, but they still keep kapooshing-out on you, which is a little humiliating, since the Country of the Bear has already had three *splendid* flights!

So, here you are! You've come from the glamour of silken gloves to the harshness of smelly earth, picking a carrot out of the ground, washing it off and *slamming* it on the counter; taking a butcher knife and *hacking* it to pieces! You watch your garden flourish, and you almost *despise* it.

All of your fortune has gone into preparation. What was it he said? "Invest in wheat futures?" Bah-humbug!

You're getting the gist of this story?

Audience: Yes.

Ramtha: Now, I wish to know how many of you—by raising your wonderful right hands—would regret the preparation if nothing ever happened? *(Seeing only a few meekly-raised hands)* Come on! *(Raises a wilting arm)* Don't do this! Reach for the heavens! Either it is a knowingness or it isn't! You would either regret it or you wouldn't! *(The hands are raised a bit more.)* Higher! *(They straighten their arms, and more audience members join them.)*

Masters, if *that* is your knowingness, in spite of all the future might bring, I advise you to do . . . *nothing*.

No matter *what* happens on the horizon, if you ever regret what you are doing, you're not going to survive anyway, because you will not be able to think or reason, because you would still be locked into a consciousness of sorrow and regret. Do you understand what I am saying?

Audience: Yes.

Ramtha: Know for yourself, absolutely. Don't do this because *I* tell you to! Whatever decision you make, it should be because it is *your* feeling and *your* knowingness; you are going forward with it and you are trusting it. Prepare because *you* want to, and take responsibility for your actions.

Now, understand this: As a god awakens and his brain begins to open beyond one-third mind, whatever he thinks has a thousand times more power to manifest than it did before. So, if you go forward and are evolving, but then, in mid-stream, you waver, because you realize that you don't really like where you are, and you start lashing out and blaming others for putting you there, that will come back to you *one thousandfold*. The greatest impact of the blame, bitterness and regret will be inside of *you*. That is where it manifests. It will comes back at you with a furiosity you have never experienced before. Never have you seen your words come back to you so quickly. Never have you felt an emotion and seen it manifest in your body within moments. Understand?

Audience: Yes.

Ramtha: Change is arduous for most. The move out of social consciousness *will* be regretful if you do not wholly embrace the change and know that through its irritation will come pearls of great wisdom. If you are going to regret it, don't do anything. Stay right where you are and go down with your ship. Never, *ever* proceed forward and blame that forward thrust on anyone! Take the responsibility that this is *your*

Never proceed forward and blame that forward thrust on anyone!

knowingness that you are enacting, a feeling that has struck a cord within your being and you are honoring it. Did I make a good point?

Audience: Yes.

Ramtha: You are God, awakening in a process of decision. An awakening master takes *full responsibility* for his actions in going forward, always cultivating and nourishing the open mind which sees neither good nor bad, only "is."

The power that acclimates itself to the opening of the brain is pure energy; it is the Is. It is neither good nor bad, perfect nor imperfect; it simply is power. And with that power, you thrust *through* the limited mind of social consciousness into an open mind; and that mind is the glorified and refined state called christus, the awakened christ.

Nothing quickens the annointment of a master greater than being faced with survival.

Nothing quickens the annointment of a master greater than being faced with survival, because then he has to call on the strength within to get him through, which allows him to help others in need. To get one's hands dirty with blood, to smell the stench of rotting bodies, open sores, and the uncleanliness of devastation—these things powerfully create the courage and humility that brims with love. Nothing ripens so many more quickly than the need to survive on one's own merit. All of a sudden, color, creed, religious and political differences, degrees of social standing, all dissolve. It is just one brother with another, in equality.

You are all gods, asleep in the dream of social consciousness, none daring enough to be an individual apart from of the mob. In survival, it is with one's knowingness and courage and desire for self-preservation that he begins to uniquely carve the character of a god from the mass of human flesh.

To look through a window of the probabilities that lie in front of you takes great courage, because to even look means you must react; and reaction means that you must change; and to change, you must draw from yourself the strength and the knowingness that allows you to push forward. To look, to react, to change—you have to take full responsibility for that. Don't get in the middle of the stream and then blame someone else because you're there. Know that it is *you* who are the one who is making that decision because you *want* to go forward into Forever.

To be God is to enact your inalienable right to move forward. The thrust to become that is called *want*, desire. And what lies on the other side of the thrust is a utopia called Superconsciousness, a collective whose whole social order will differ drastically from what you know it to be now. It will be a society where there are no boundaries or demarcation lines, where there is understanding and knowledge of the most grand proportion taking place in a mind that was cultured to allow it to happen. It takes a very strong, very humble entity to go against the grain of social consciousness and move forward into Superconsciousness—to move into tomorrow without the regret of yesterday. Get it?

It takes a very strong, very humble entity to go against the grain of social consciousness and move forward into tomorrow without the regret of yesterday.

Audience: Yes.

Ramtha: Now, if you raised your hand before, I give unto you the wisdom that says, "Do *nothing*." Otherwise, you will only become more miserable and confused than you now are. To the rest of you, if this truth rings within your soul and it is inspiring to you, and you own up to your part played in this grand eclipse of Nature, then go forward. But always know that you are doing so because you *want* to. Ask yourself: "What if, by the grace of Nature, the elements do not convulse and eclipse? What would I feel then? Would I be disappointed, regretful, sorrowful? Would I be angry, spiteful? Would I go back into the fickle mob whence I came?" Go through these emotions and embrace the truth within you. Feel, feel, *feel*, until you have purged these things from your being. Polish your knowingness until it is like a sword that is clean, brilliant and swift.

Reason everything that I have taught you to its most infinite understanding—from right to wrong, to the understanding that sits in the center, called Is. That is the understanding called Forever. When you can look through the window from the centerpoint of your emotions, you'll know precisely what to do. You will look at the future, not as good or bad, but as a continuum of adventure. You shan't waver or doubt yourself, which destroys the thrust forward. You shall be in the center, called *knowingness*, and there, you can never regret your movement forward.

If you can't get to the center focal point, ask and reason with yourself, "*Why* haven't I made peace with this? Why have I allowed myself to be confused?" Then allow the answer as to *why* you're not moving, *why* you aren't acting, to come forth from within you. Then ask yourself, "Is it worth losing myself because of this 'why-factor'?" If it is, stay where you are. Be true to yourself and stay! Because in *your* truth, that is your comfort zone, and that, indeed, is what you *can* live with.

I have said—and it is a great truth—that there is only a handful of entities who have the desire and the courage to go forward. The majority of you are too vain for discovery.

You are not expected to do anything.

Now, it is important to know that you are not *expected* to do *anything*. Regardless of what you do, you are loved and nurtured by God and Life because you are important, you are part of the Is, you are brothers unto the living Source. Even asleep in the dream, you are still loved. Whatever your decisions are, don't be ashamed of them. Own them. Realize that they're *your* decisions. Nothing that you do can lose you favor, if you will, in the eyes of God. Always, you are the apple of God's eye. If mankind could have ever earned condemnation for his antics, humanity would have been done away with eons ago. But miraculously, the species of cellular mass, called humanoid, has survived.

Many times in your historical evolution, mankind has been divinely intervened upon to salvage his perpetual self from the carelessness of his ignorance, stupidity, and debased spiritual acts. Why have you been *worth* salvaging? Why, if your spirit, soul and ego live in a forever cycle to play out your dreams and realities—why, then, is man, the species of flesh and blood worth salvaging? Because flesh-and-blood is also the miraculous God, called Life, and *its* natural destiny is to live forever. Did you know that? Every cell in your body has divine intelligence. Every cell has a soul, because without the soul to hold the entire physiological pattern for your refurbishment, your body could never regenerate.

You have been allowed the instrument of flesh and blood so that you you can delve into the adventures of this dimension. But what you, the god who sits upon the body's throne, have been doing to your body is that which prohibits its natural evolution, its forever destiny. You have *chosen* to be human, but you have forgotten the importance in being here. You have chosen to merge with the density of coagulated thought that is called flesh and blood. The spectacular god that you are has chosen the most hard-pressed realizaton there is, an adventure that pits you against the plane of demonstrated mass. You have chosen this adventure, but are stuck in the dream of what is real and what is *un*real, because the adventure allows you to limit yourself all the way into a sphere of decadence and the inward collapse of the soul. *(Toasts)* To realities!

Audience: To realities.

Ramtha: All of you have taken on the adventure that angels fear to tread. Know you an angel? It is only pure energy without the experiences and adventures that ripen it into wisdom and help define the understanding called forever. "Angels fear to tread" is an apropos statement, because in mass, there is the distinct possibility that a god can close down so much of its mind that it collapses inwardly into unresolved thought, a limbo situation.

Now, the body is, indeed, "earth-to-earth and ashes-to-ashes." But it can be easily resurrected, over and over and over again. What is arduous to resurrect is an entity bent on his own self-destruction. If God could ever pit himself against himself in a fencing duel, he has most certainly done it here, in the vibrance and the cunning of humanity.

If God could ever pit himself against himself in a fencing duel, he has most certainly done it here, in the vibrance and the cunning of humanity.

Not all of the thrust of billions of suns can open a mind that is determined to stay closed. Knowledge is the movement within you that allows you wake up and to go into Forever. But the way "into" is determined *from within*. Through your *desire*, through your *allowing*, you wholly determine how much you know or don't know.

In this three-dimensional understanding, Nature is the only reality that exists. But mankind has lost that understanding because he has been living in a dream, perpetuated by eons of illusions. What is *real* is what you put your feet on! what you breathe! the seasons of fruit and plenty and sweet slumber. *That* is reality. That is pure and simple, and it will live forever, with or without you.

One who wakes up, flows with Nature; he is in a harmonious movement with it liken unto a symphony. And it takes only a *little* to understand and become that way . . . so little. Those who are pitted against the rallying point of survival, and then bloom from the experience, are truly God, magnified throughout the whole of Life. They have gone against enormous odds to awaken from a dream so deep that when one does awaken, there is no measure to his treasure of understanding. In that understanding, there lies no sorrow or tears, no admonishment, no punishment, no suffering. There lies only Life in the most extraordinary, awaiting manner. When that happens, the whole of Forever changes; the whole of Life has been enriched because there is another part of God who has gone *into* mass and then awakened *through* mass into the frequency of joy, wholly bloomed.

The whole of life has been enriched because there is another part of God who has gone into mass and then awakened through mass into the frequency of joy, wholly bloomed.

I love what you are. I respect your opinions and love you for it. But I want you to know that there is a *reason* that you are here; that you chose to come here to complete your understanding of God, because only through flesh and blood is a christ born. Perhaps now you will contemplate the importance and the *magnitude* of that divine step into mass, called mankind—humanity.

You are a divine lot. All along, you thought you were the worst, the lowest plane, the densest, the "outpost of Forever." You thought that whatever is on the ethereal plane is much better than you. Well, the reverse it true. When you wake up, you'll know that.

This that I have taught to you is perhaps an arduous understanding. But if it was more than you could aspire to, I would not have spoken it. Never. You are a maturing species; and in that maturity, you are coming to a point where you will become more mobile, focused, aligned, and knowing—to the zenith of your comprehension.

If you need direction, speak from the lord-god of your being and ask that the answers come forward. You will feel a knowingness that comes and grabs you with great emotion. That is how you will know that answer that will allow you to go forward and become greater.

Now, go and contemplate the knowledge I have engaged you with here. Contemplate your tenuous, little body that houses a great god, and think about why two-thirds of your brain is asleep. In the midst of that, have some jolly good food and a jolly drink. If you've never really savored food before, savor it! If you've never realized the wonderment of wine going down your gullet, realize it! Then go and think, and just be. I will be with all of you, for I will be the wind at your backs. I love you. So be it.

***

SOVEREIGNTY CARRIES ALL RAMTHA BOOKS • AUDIO TAPES • VIDEO TAPES

Call or write us for a complete catalog or order through your local bookstore.

Ramtha. Edited by Steven Lee Weinberg, Ph.D., this critically acclaimed best seller presents the cornerstones of Ramtha's teachings. Called by Ramtha "The Great White Book," it is impeccably edited and beautifully designed. More than 75,000 copies have been sold since it was published in March, 1986. *Sovereignty.*

Highest quality hardcover $19.95
Special leatherbound edition $29.95

Ramtha: An Introduction. Edited by Steven Lee Weinberg, this multi-faceted book engages the emotions, challenges the mind, and touches the heart. More than an introduction, this superbly edited book conveys the full spectrum of Ramtha's teachings and will be of great value even to those already familiar with the teachings. Published October, 1987. *Sovereignty.*

Quality trade paperback $9.95

A State Of Mind, My Story: Ramtha, The Adventure Begins. Written by JZ Knight, this is the first volume of her autobiography in which she engagingly recounts her life and her involvement with Ramtha. Published October, 1987. *Warner Books.*

Hardcover $15.95

I Am Ramtha. A stunning photo essay of Ramtha and JZ Knight with accompanying teachings. Published May, 1986. *Beyond Words.*

Hardcover $24.95

Audience With Ramtha. The most popular video, this is a warm, intimate, and colorful presentation of Ramtha's teachings on relationships, passion, living happily, drugs, the science of thought, and much more. As the only video of a Ramtha Dialogue, is presents Ramtha's teachings through the question-and-answer format, and includes a rare interview with JZ Knight. Edited from the audience presented in Honolulu on July 14-15, 1984. *Indeed Productions.*

2 Video tapes $90

Ramtha And His Teachings. An introduction to Ramtha's teachings in a video format, this tape is composed of edited excerpts from the video tape series. Teachings include the meaning and process of enlightenment, the effects of drugs on the body, and coming changes in the environment and in society. *Ramtha Dialogues.*

1 Video tape $48

Ramtha Intensive: Soulmates. The first volume of the Intensive Series, this book is an edited transcript of the Seattle Intensive of January 10-12, 1986. It is a passionate teaching on the science of soulmates, the degradation of male-female relationships that has kept soulmates apart, and the reunion of soulmates through the power of love. Published September, 1987. *Sovereignty.*

Quality paperback $10

Voyage To The New World. Written by Douglas James Mahr, this book is a collection of Ramtha's teachings, commentaries on the teachings and the phenomenon of channeling, and interviews with JZ Knight and other individuals who have grown through their association with Ramtha. Published 1985. *Masterworks.*

Quality paperback $9.95

Becoming, A Master's Manual. Edited by Khit Harding, this attractive publication is a collection of quotes from Ramtha's teachings. Published 1986. *Adams Publishing.*

Quality paperback $14.95

"Windwords." A monthly newspaper featuring reports about recent Ramtha Intensives, informative articles, a calendar of Ramtha events, information on self-sufficiency programs, networking information, and more. 1 year subscription for US and Canada is $24 (foreign $28). Contact *"Windwords"* directly to subscribe: Box 576, Rainier, WA 98576.

RECOMMENDED MATERIAL RELATED TO NATURE AND EARTH CHANGES

Winds of Change. Select teachings elaborating on coming changing in the earth, the economy, and society. Edited from an audience presented in Yelm, WA in July, 1987. *Ramtha Dialogues.*

1 Audio tape $8

Change: The Days To Come. The audio and video recordings of the Intensive that this book was based on. *Ramtha Dialogues.*

5 Audio tapes $40
4 Video tapes $160

The Meek Will Inherit: The Days To Come. Presented by Ramtha in Tampa on May 10-11, 1986, this was the first Intensive devoted entirely to earth changes and personal sovereignty. *Ramtha Dialogues.*

6 Audio tapes $48

Survival: The Power To Manifest. In this Intensive, presented in Seattle on November 8-9, 1986, Ramtha discusses the barriers we've erected that inhibit the free flow of abundance, health, and fulfillment. Contains an effective teaching on how to apply the science of manifestation to create your days to come. *Ramtha Dialogues.*

5 Audio Tapes $40
4 Video tapes $160

Note: Audio tapes are normally 90 minutes in length. Video tapes are approximately 2 hours in length. Please specify Beta or VHS when ordering video tapes.

TO PLACE YOUR ORDER CALL
1-800-654-1407 or 1-800-356-5483

In Washington and Alaska call collect 206-376-2177

Shipping And Handling: All orders are shipped UPS unless First Class Mail is requested. No Charge for orders totaling $40 or more. For orders under $40, add $2.75. (Hawaii and Alaska, add $4.75.) Foreign orders, please call or write for rates.

Sales Tax: Washington state residents, add 7.5% sales tax to total.

Money Back Guarantee: The full price of any book or tape (less shipping charges) will be immediately refunded if you are not completely satisfied with your purchase for any reason. Items must be returned in resaleable condition within 30 days of our shipping date.

Sovereignty, Box 926, Eastsound, WA 98245